Composite Predicates in Late Modern English

This volume provides a concise overview of the diachronic development of composite predicates (CPs) in Late Modern English, offering clearer evidence of ongoing language change using data less readily available in other corpora.

While previous scholarship on CPs exists from a synchronic perspective, this book is the first to focus exclusively on Late Modern English with a diachronic approach to CPs, understood as phraseological verbs consisting of a verb and a deverbal noun or this combination with a preposition, such as *to ask a question* or *to take hold of*. The volume builds on real-life spoken data encompassing the proceedings of the Old Bailey at the Central Criminal Court in London, which predate the invention of audio-recording technology. Leone explores syntactic and semantic changes and the role performed by phenomena associated with grammaticalization, lexicalization, and idiomatization in this period from both quantitative and qualitative perspectives.

The book sheds light on ongoing processes of change in spoken data, enriching knowledge on language change in this period and offering directions for future research. This book will appeal to scholars in English historical linguistics, syntax and semantics, and language change.

Ljubica Leone is currently a postdoctoral fellow at the University of Milan, Italy. She earned her PhD in Literary and Linguistic Studies from the University of Salerno, Italy.

Routledge Focus on Linguistics

Linguistic Description in English for Academic Purposes
Helen Basturkmen

Antonyms in Mind and Brain
Evidence from English and German
Sandra Kotzor

Picturing Fiction through Embodied Cognition
Drawn Representations and Viewpoint in Literary Texts
Bien Klomberg, Theresa Schilhab, and Michael Burke

The Discursive Construction of the Modern Political Self
Alexandria Ocasio-Cortez in the Age of Social Media
Jacqueline Aiello

Using AI for Dialoguing with Texts
From Psychology to Cinema and Literature
Yair Neuman, Marcel Danesi, and Dan Vilenchik

Composite Predicates in Late Modern English
Ljubica Leone

For more information about this series, please visit: www.routledge.com/Routledge-Focus-on-Linguistics/book-series/RFL

Composite Predicates in Late Modern English

Ljubica Leone

NEW YORK AND LONDON

First published 2024
by Routledge
605 Third Avenue, New York, NY 10158

and by Routledge
4 Park Square, Milton Park, Abingdon, Oxon, OX14 4RN

Routledge is an imprint of the Taylor & Francis Group, an informa business

© 2024 Ljubica Leone

The right of Ljubica Leone to be identified as author of this work has been asserted in accordance with sections 77 and 78 of the Copyright, Designs and Patents Act 1988.

All rights reserved. No part of this book may be reprinted or reproduced or utilised in any form or by any electronic, mechanical, or other means, now known or hereafter invented, including photocopying and recording, or in any information storage or retrieval system, without permission in writing from the publishers.

Trademark notice: Product or corporate names may be trademarks or registered trademarks, and are used only for identification and explanation without intent to infringe.

Library of Congress Cataloging-in-Publication Data
Names: Leone, Ljubica, author.
Title: Composite predicates in late modern English / Ljubica Leone.
Description: New York, NY : Routledge, 2024. |
Series: Routledge focus on linguistics |
Includes bibliographical references and index. |
Identifiers: LCCN 2024014937 |
Subjects: LCSH: English language–Verb phrase. |
English language–Syntax. | Linguistic change. |
English language–Grammar, Historical. | English language–18th century. |
English language–19th century.
Classification: LCC PE1319 .L46 2024 |
DDC 425/.6–dc23/eng/20240407
LC record available at https://lccn.loc.gov/2024014937

ISBN: 9781032524887 (hbk)
ISBN: 9781032530956 (pbk)
ISBN: 9781003410256 (ebk)

DOI: 10.4324/9781003410256

Typeset in Times New Roman
by Newgen Publishing UK

Contents

List of figures — vii
List of tables — viii
Acknowledgments — ix
List of abbreviations and conventions — x

1 Composite predicates in 1750–1850 — 1
   1.1 Background 1
   1.2 Linguistic overview of composite predicates 4
   1.3 Previous studies and research aims 6
   1.4 The corpus: the Late Modern English-Old Bailey Corpus 7
      1.4.1 Corpus compilation: source data, sampling, text types 7
      1.4.2 Corpus architecture and size 9
   1.5 Method: selectional criteria, corpus-based techniques, and statistical tests 10
      1.5.1 Selection of CPs 10
      1.5.2 Concordance-based analysis of selected CPs 11
      1.5.3 Quantitative analysis 11
   1.6 The structure of the book 12

2 History — 14
   2.1 Old English and Middle English: the establishment of composite predicates 14
   2.2 Early Modern English: the spread of composite predicates 18

- 2.3 Late Modern English: stability and change 21
- 2.4 Present Day English: current forms and uses 23

3 Linguistic features 25
- 3.1 Distribution of composite predicates 25
- 3.2 The base verbs 30
- 3.3 Phrasal profile and productivity of composite predicates 31
  - 3.3.1 Phraseological variation across the years 1750–1850 31
  - 3.3.2 The use of deverbal nouns with more than one verb 34
  - 3.3.3 Productivity 37

4 Composite predicates between stability and change 41
- 4.1 Stable composite predicates 41
- 4.2 Morpho-syntactic features of composite predicate 42
  - 4.2.1 Syntactic patterns 42
  - 4.2.2 Articles and determiners 44
  - 4.2.3 Internal modification 47
  - 4.2.4 The use of plural forms 50
  - 4.2.5 Passivization 51
- 4.3 Semantic features 53

5 Processes of change 55
- 5.1 Grammaticalization and lexicalization 55
- 5.2 Phraseological variation and layering between alternative prepositions 59
- 5.3 The coinage of new composite predicates 61
- 5.4 Semantic change 64

6 Conclusion 67

Appendix: list of composite predicates 70
References 73
Index 81

Figures

1.1	Clines of lexicality and grammaticality	4
3.1	Composite predicates over the years 1750–1850 (Nf per 1,000 words)	27
3.2	Linear regression over the years 1750–1850	28
3.3	Light verbs over the years 1750–1850 (Nf per 1,000 words)	30

Tables

1.1	Corpus architecture and size	9
3.1	Some nouns occurring in composite predicates	33
3.2	Top composite predicates of each base verb: Raw frequency	33
3.3	*Have care/take care* and *have use/make use*: Raw frequency over the decades	36
3.4	Type/Token Ratio of base verbs	38
3.5	Type/Token Ratio of base verbs per decade	39
4.1	Articles and determiners of composite predicates (%)	45
4.2	Modification of composite predicates (%)	47
4.3	Percentages of singular nouns in EModE and LModE	50
4.4	Passive form (%) and raw frequency (n)	52

Acknowledgments

The study presented in the present book aims to offer a comprehensive account of the linguistic features and processes of changes affecting composite predicates over the Late Modern period, specifically during the years 1750–1850. Adopting a corpus-based methodology, composite predicates have been examined as complex lexemes characterized by a phraseological structure which is the result of intertwining processes of change that have been operative since the Old English period.

Since the completion of my PhD, I have devoted my interest to the diachronic aspects of the English verb system and mechanisms of change, focusing especially on phrasal verbs, prepositional verbs, phrasal-prepositional verbs, and verb-adjective combinations. Reading the literature on composite predicates raised my interest in these verbs, and stimulated the need for a monograph with an exclusive focus on them.

Many people have contributed to the research presented in this monograph. Any errors are mine. I would like to thank Elly van Gelderen, Merja Kytö, Nikolaos Lavidas, and the anonymous reviewers for their comments and suggestions for improvement. I would like to thank the editors of the Routledge Focus Series for their support throughout all stages of the writing process, and the technical team who worked on the final layout of the book. A special thank you to the audience of the ICAME 44 Conference for discussion and feedback on part of the study included in the monograph. Finally, a special mention is reserved for my family, all my colleagues, and my friends.

Abbreviations and conventions

ARCHER	*A Representative Corpus of Historical English Registers*
Art	article
CED	*Corpus of English Dialogues*
CP	composite predicate
D	determiner
Diff%	difference expressed in percentages
EModE	Early Modern English
LL	log-likelihood
LModE	Late Modern English
LModE-OBC	*Late Modern English-Old Bailey Corpus*
ME	Middle English
MED	*Middle English Dictionary*
N	noun
Nf	normalized frequency
OBC	*Old Bailey Corpus*
OE	Old English
OED	*Oxford English Dictionary*
OTA	*Oxford Text Archive*
PDE	Present Day English
P	preposition
Pp	personal pronoun
Rf	raw frequency
TTR	type/token ratio
V	verb

1 Composite predicates in 1750–1850

1.1 Background

Composite predicates (hereafter CPs) are phraseological verbs consisting of a verb (V) plus a deverbal noun (N) which behave as a single lexical unit (Quirk et al. 1985; Biber et al. 1999, 2021). Linguistically, CPs occur in the form verb (+ article) + deverbal noun, e.g. *give an answer*, as in (1), or in the form verb (+ article) + deverbal noun + preposition, for example, *take part of*, *pay attention to*, as in (2)–(3).

(1) I considered some time before I **gave an answer**, but I did not say I was not quite sure about it. (1810s)[1]
(2) I met him, and asked him to go and **take part of** a pint of porter. (1810s)
(3) You **paid no attention to** the persons who went down to the left side? (1790s)

CPs such as *give an answer*, *take part of*, and *pay attention to* work as prototypical examples of this verb group despite being different in terms of constituency: the bases *have* and *take* occur with a very general or no meaning and, when combined with the nominal part, work as prototypical examples of multi-word verbs.

Multi-word verbs include various groups formed by two or more words that exhibit a lexeme status (Quirk et al. 1985; Biber et al. 1999, 2021; Huddleston & Pullum 2002): (i) phrasal verbs (e.g. *set up*), as in (4); (ii) prepositional verbs (e.g. *deal with*), as in (5); (iii) phrasal-prepositional verbs (e.g. *get on with*), as in (6); (iv) verb-verb combinations (e.g. *let go*), as in (7); (v) verb-prepositional phrase

DOI: 10.4324/9781003410256-1

combinations (e.g. *put in mind*), as in (8); (vi) verb-adjective combinations (e.g. *break open*), as in (9):

(4) On the night of the 11th of December, and the morning of the 12th, I **set up** till between one and two o'clock. (1750s)
(5) The prisoner had **dealt with** me for a long period, and after long importuning on his part for a job, I gave him a pair of shoes and boots to mend. (1810s)
(6) he asked how I **got on with** them? (1810s)
(7) there is a girl gone by with a bundle, **let us go** and snatch it from her. (1790s)
(8) Did you **put** his father and mother **in mind** you had been in the room the night before? (1770s)
(9) we tried **to break open** the windows but could not get them open. (1770s)

Examples (4)–(9), in comparison with those reported in (1)–(3), prove that all multi-word verbs are characterized by a polylexical constituency, that is, they operate as phraseological forms: indeed, following Gries (2008: 6), a phraseologism is "the co-occurrence of a form or a lemma of a lexical item and one or more detailed linguistic elements of various kinds which functions as one semantic unit in a clause or sentence and whose frequency of co-occurrence is larger than expected on the basis of change."

All these verb groups have common histories that go back to the tendency towards analyticity attested in early times in English, which favored increasing segmentalization of instances (Danchev 1992; Brinton 1996; Brinton & Akimoto 1999). A widely shared idea is that CPs underwent a process leading to the splitting of the verb into two parts (Live 1973: 31), and this resulted in the establishment of CPs as they are known today. A partly shared path of development, which features the grammaticalization of adjacent words and their univerbation as a single lexeme, explains the existence of overlapping characteristics concerning both the syntactic and semantic levels. For example, all multi-word verbs are affected by limited flexibility, unitary status in the passive transformation and, semantically, in many cases, non-compositional meanings.

The phraseological constituency of CPs has given rise to many diverse designations with names such as "composite predicates" (Cattell 1984), "complex verbs" (Olsson 1961; Nickel 1968), "verbal phrases" (Hiltunen 1999), and "verbo-nominal combinations" (Claridge 2000), all emphasizing the periphrastic substance of CPs. Indeed, these verbs emerged as polylexical instances, often behaving as single idiomatic units (Quirk et al. 1985: 1530n). Polylexicality is a key issue in the evaluation of the linguistic status of CPs since it is one of the conditions that determine the attribution of a phraseological status to instances (Granger & Paquot 2008: 32) while functioning as a factor in support of the idea that CPs stand "somewhere near the middle of the magnetic field of language [...] where grammar and lexis meet" (Algeo 1995: 203). The examination of multi-word verbs like CPs inevitably raises questions about the link between lexis and syntax, which was first postulated back in 1991 by Sinclair (1991: 104) claiming that "the decoupling of lexis and syntax leads to the creation of a rubbish dump" known as "phraseology." The phraseological status of combinations exhibiting fixedness in form and often idiosyncrasy (Svensson 2008: 82) reveals the double nature of CPs emerging linguistically from the intersection between a grammatical side linked to the degree of separateness of their constituents and a lexical one deriving from their lexeme status (Brinton 2008: 36). Indeed, CPs are verbs that behave Janus-like, that is, they work as syntactic constructions but also single lexical units (Algeo 1995: 204; see Brinton 2008: 36).

Following the functional approach to the study of language (Hopper & Traugott 2003; Brinton & Traugott 2005; Fischer 2007), instances can move towards a more "grammatical" or more "lexical" status (Brinton & Traugott 2005: 101); this means that CPs may be seen as instances that may be diachronically placed anywhere between the lexical/grammatical pole, and that they may be grammaticalized/lexicalized to different degrees.

Typically, lexicalization involves fusion and univerbation of components, phonological coalescence, and increasing semantic idiomaticity, whereas grammaticalization prompts the acquisition of a more bounded grammatical status to affected instances then working as functional/grammatical forms, which may become "semantic contentless i.e. bleached, and even non-referential" items (Brinton & Traugott 2005: 97, 99). Moreover, considering that within functional linguistics language change is conceptualized as a gradual process (Fischer 2007: 75), grammaticalization should be intended as the process rendering a unit more "grammatical/functional/productive" (G1>G2>G3), as represented in Figure 1.1 below. At the same time,

4 Composite predicates in 1750–1850

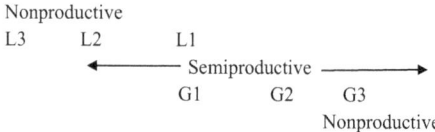

Figure 1.1 Clines of lexicality and grammaticality.

lexicalization turns out to be the process that makes a unit more "lexical/contentful/nonproductive" (L1>L2>L3) (Brinton & Traugott 2005:101). There is a cline of grammaticality and lexicality, and single forms may be placed anywhere in their process of development and move from a semiproductive (L1 and G1) to productive (G3) or, conversely, nonproductive (L3) pole, as represented by Brinton and Traugott (2005: 102) with a schema that has been revised and reported in Figure 1.1.

In this view, CPs may work as grammaticalized verbs on some occasions (Brinton & Akimoto 1999), but as lexicalized or semi-lexicalized lexemes in others (Traugott 1999; Claridge 2000). This means that CPs should be examined by looking at the unitary status within the constituents, which may reveal grammaticalization and/or increasing lexicalization but also variation in their phrasal profile, that is, variation of the nominal part, interchangeability of the base verb, or occurrence of an additional preposition. Moreover, CPs should be examined as instances that are variously affected by semantic reanalysis, that is, innovation of their semantic shades, or idiomatization leading towards non-compositionality. Similar to other multi-word verbs, there could be cases of analogy intended as the "generalization or optimization of a rule from a relatively limited domain to a far broader one" (Hopper & Traugott 2003: 64), which can determine the establishment of new members of CPs by means of direct formation: a verb+noun combination can emerge by taking already established CPs as their models to follow. In this case, a well-established CP may work as a model to follow and stimulate the coinage of new members of this verb group.

1.2 Linguistic overview of composite predicates

CPs can be classified into three groups depending on whether the preposition must occur as part of the combination or whether, instead, it is optional: (i) V (+ article) + N, as (10); (ii) V (+ article) + N + P, as in (11); (iii) CPs that occur both with and without a preposition, as in (12)–(13):

(10) I do not remember **making her any answer**, but I got 1d. worth of string, and some brownpaper to tie the desk up again. (1810s)
(11) "That is nothing to you, I'll tell your master" – he **gave no account of** himself in my hearing. (1810s)
(12) She said, no, Sir; but pray why do you **make this enquiry of** me. (1790s)
(13) I **made enquiry**, and found that the prosecutor had lost these things, and he came forward and swore to them. (1790s)

All these groups are characterized by internal flexibility and internal variation concerning the presence/absence of the determiner before the noun, e.g. *have a walk* vs. *take place*, or the occurrence of a preposition following the verb + noun combination, e.g. *take care of*.

Syntactically, many CPs allow adjectival modification of the noun, topicalization, and diverse options of passivization. Specifically, there are two types of the passive form (Brinton 2011): (i) the *inner* passive, that is, the deverbal noun becomes the subject of the passive, "*thought was given to the design*, but not **the design was given thought*"; (ii) the *outer* passive, that is, the object of the preposition becomes the subject of the passive, for example, "*advice was given to her/she was given advice*)" (Brinton 2011: 561). The syntactic behavior is a direct consequence of the peculiar morphological status of the combinations, which also determines the semantics of CPs.

Specifically, CPs are morphologically defined as verbs characterized by a tripartite structure consisting of a base, that is, *do*, *give*, *have*, *make*, and *take*, which is followed by an article and a deverbative noun that may be phonologically or derivationally linked to the "corresponding verbal stem, e.g. *have a shower/shower*" (Brinton & Akimoto 1999: 2). The deverbal noun, also referred to as "eventive object," works as the semantic focus of the verb and conveys most of the meaning (Quirk et al. 1985: 750). The verb in CPs carries little meaning and performs a connective function (Brinton 2011: 560): it is linguistically dependent on the following elements, and "the semantic weight of the combination is disrupted, with the verbal notion displaced from the verb itself onto the postverbal element" (Brinton & Akimoto

1999: 5; see Algeo 1995). In this view, the base verb "is almost devoid of lexical meaning but embodies the associated grammatical information" whereas the noun "carries the lexical load, conveying verb-like meaning, although its form is not that of a verb" (Live 1973: 31). This renders the base verb as an empty or "light verb" (Live 1973: 31; see Cattell 1984) which is semantically dependent on the nominal part working as the semantic centre (Brinton 1996: 187; see Live 1973; Algeo 1995). This is a prominent feature of CPs formed with *do*, *give*, *have*, *make*, and *take*, which combine with nouns to form one single verb working as a phraseological unit.

The internal cohesion between the base verb and the following noun along with the semantic dependency between the constituents is further corroborated by the paradigmatic competition that often occurs between CPs and simple verbs exhibiting the same meanings, such as *have a talk* vs *talk* (Brinton & Akimoto 1999; Kytö 1999). If substitutability is a "diagnostic tool for recognizing synonyms" (Murphy 2003: 159) and a prerequisite for the phraseological status of combinations (Svensson 2008), then CPs may be classified as verbs with a complex internal characterization: they are multi-word lexemes that have emerged over time through several intertwining processes and mechanisms, and diachronically were closed to other English multi-word verbs.

1.3 Previous studies and research aims

Much scholarship has been undertaken on CPs from a variety of perspectives to examine the aspects concerning their morphological status (Curme 1931; Quirk et al. 1985; Algeo 1995), their grammatical functions (Quirk et al. 1985; Algeo 1995; Biber et al. 1999), and their semantic substance (Live 1973; Matsumoto 2007; Rayson 2008). Most of this work, however, has focused on synchronic features of CPs. Diachronic investigations, in contrast, have described the development of CPs in early times, often disregarding the more recent history of English.

CPs of early periods have been examined as being part of verbal phrases by Nickel (1968), or described as independent classes of verbs by Hiltunen (1983), and Denison (1981), who highlight the ability of CPs to form alternative passives. CPs originated in Old English (OE) (Hiltunen 1983; Akimoto & Brinton 1999), and since then "evolved gradually in the Middle English period" (Akimoto & Brinton 1999: 21). They are, nonetheless, recurrent in Early Modern English (EModE) (Görlach 1991; Hiltunen 1999; Kytö 1999; Claridge 2000), and were still involved in processes of renewal, especially affecting their semantic features. A common position shared by many historical works is that CPs increased their nominal constituents during the Middle English (ME) period (Brinton & Traugott 2005: 130; see Iglesias-Rábade 2001; Moralejo Gárate 2002), which was a determinant step towards the fixedness of instances and to the increasing idiomaticity also during EModE time (Claridge 2000: 95; see Kytö 1999).

CPs of the LModE period, in contrast, have been approached with a descriptive perspective, mainly to identify the shift from the synthetic to the analytic tendency of the language, or with a focus on the idiomatic properties (Akimoto 1999; Matsumoto 2008). In this respect, grammaticalization and lexicalization, which were sometimes followed by idiomatization, are the processes that played a major role in the development of multi-word verbs from early times (Denison 1981; Elenbaas 2007; Thim 2012; Leone 2023) up to more modern periods (Akimoto 1989, 1999; Matsumoto 2008).

Starting from these considerations, the present study aims to contribute to existing knowledge on the processes of change of CPs and contextualizes the discussion within studies on CPs and multi-word verbs from OE to PDE. Specifically, the present research examines (i) the distributional properties of CPs in 1750–1850; (ii) the degree of productivity of CPs; (iii) the linguistic features and uses of CPs; (iv) the phraseological variation and interchangeability of verbs with a common object, for example, *to {take/have} a drink*; (v) the role of grammaticalization, lexicalization, idiomatization, direct formation and analogy in the evolution of CPs.

1.4 The corpus: the *Late Modern English-Old Bailey Corpus*

1.4.1 Corpus compilation: source data, sampling, text types

The study discussed in the present monograph has been undertaken by combining the phraseological approach (Sinclair 1991) with corpus linguistics. The study is based on the purpose-built corpus called the *Late Modern English-Old Bailey Corpus* (*LModE-OBC*) which includes witness depositions that were given and trials that were held at the Old Bailey, London's Central Criminal Court. The corpus includes more than one million words and texts recorded during the years 1750–1850.

The *LModE-OBC* consists of samples of proceedings which are freely accessible online at www.oldbaileyonline.org/. This website is a repository of proceedings recorded from 1674 to 1913 and allows different kinds of searches based on the personal details of speakers, crime, punishment sentences, and surname of speakers (Huber 2007). Moreover, it also gives access to the transcriptions of trials selected by date, which was one of the major aspects driving methodological choices in the phase of corpus compilation.

The proceedings[2] can be used for both historical and linguistic research: they contain detailed descriptions of crimes and criminal justice and provide information on habits from past times while also being a source of transcriptions that are very accurate (Huber 2007). Indeed, they have been used in studies ranging from examination of trade networks and riots (Baker 2016, 2017) to detectives (Beattie 2012) and the welfare system (Boulton 2007). At the same time, many works examine the language used in the Old Bailey courtroom, which cover topics including pragmatic and sociolinguistic features of degree modifiers (Claridge & Kytö 2014), sociolinguistic variation in the use of relativizers (Huber 2017), and diachronic aspects of the English verb system, phrasal verbs (Leone 2016a, 2016b) and multi-word verbs (Leone 2023). Following the historical pragmatics framework, the study of early speech taken down in writing or even fictional speech imitating authentic speech may give access to invaluable data for linguistic analysis (Culpeper & Kytö 2010). Overall, the materials are "well suited for studies within historical sociolinguistic and historical pragmatics approaches" because they include speech-related data, that is, texts belonging to the "speech-based genres," "varieties originating in speech that have been permanently preserved in writing" (Biber & Finegan 1992: 689; see Jucker 1995; Fitzmaurice & Taavitsainen 2007). Thus, despite some limitations deriving from shorthand techniques and transcription conventions (Kytö & Walker 2003; Huber 2007), speech-based genres like the proceedings are considered among the most powerful sources for linguistic research devoted to the diachronic study of the spoken dimension (Hundt 2014; Culpeper & Kytö 2010). This is a very informative dimension in language change given that it is likely to provide evidence of the beginning of a process of innovation, which is first attested in the spoken dimension. The use of speech-based genres may be debated considering that the transcriptions are made by scribes, who can be very formulaic and conservative in their writing habits. At the same time, scribes can adopt various techniques that can affect the reliability of the transcriptions (Huber 2007). However, the language reported is not pre-planned, and preserves interactivity, shared context, and expressive functions that are typically associated with spoken language from past times (Culpeper & Kytö 2010).

1.4.2 Corpus architecture and size

The *LModE-OBC* (1750–1850) is informed by the current debate on corpus compilation concerning representativeness, balance, sampling frames, and opportunistic decisions that are often necessary when designing and building a corpus (Biber 1993; Biber et al. 1998; McEnery & Hardie 2012; Ädel 2021). The corpus has been compiled to represent spoken language used in trials between the years 1750–1850, and texts were selected with a stratified sampling frame based on time: random sampling of texts was undertaken in each of the decades included in the corpus. The use of a research design based on random sampling has the advantage of preserving objectivity in the selection and controlling any bias that emerges during the compilation (Brezina 2018). Each decade was set to include around 100,000 words, which renders the results comparable even with the use of only raw figures. The *LModE-OBC* architecture and size are included in Table 1.1.

Table 1.1 Corpus architecture and size

Time	Conventional name	No. of words
1750–1769	1750s	201,533
1770–1789	1770s	201,562
1790–1809	1790s	201,770
1810–1829	1810s	201,614
1830–1849	1830s	201,755
Total no. of words		1,008,234

Using data from the *LModE-OBC* can allow the evaluation of changes in the use of CPs over the period 1750–1850. Moreover, comparative analysis of the decades permits the identification of ongoing signs of expansion or retraction in the use of CPs as well as quantification across the decades also with the support of statistical measures (see §1.5).

The data obtained by querying the *LModE-OBC* also benefits from the discussion of examples taken from *A Representative Corpus of Historical English Registers* (*ARCHER*),[3] which is a multi-genre corpus of British and American English covering the period 1600–1999; it was first compiled by Douglas Biber and Edward Finegan in the 1990s (Yáñez-Bouza 2011a, 2011b). Given the diachronic nature of the corpus, it provides data comparable with other studies attested in literature: (i) Kytö's work (1999) examining CPs occurring in the Early Modern English section of the *Helsinki Corpus of English Texts*; (ii) Wang's study (2019) querying the *Corpus of English Dialogues* between the years 1560 and 1760; (iii) works such as those undertaken by Claridge (2000), Tanabe (1999), Brinton (2008), Wang (2019) covering EModE or other periods.

1.5 Method: selectional criteria, corpus-based techniques, and statistical tests

1.5.1 Selection of CPs

Following most studies on CPs (Hiltunen 1999; Kytö 1999; Akimoto 1999), and adopting the selectional criteria defined by Kytö (1999) in her study on CPs of EModE, the analysis has been restricted to combinations formed by *do*, *give*, *have*, *make*, and *take*, which include (i) nouns that "also occur or have, as far as we know, occurred as simple verbs" (Kytö 1999: 169), or (ii) nouns that are derivationally linked to simple verbs. In the first case, there are verbs like *do harm*, as in (15), which consists of the noun *harm* also working as a verb since OE. The occurrence of a simple verb in one of the periods of English (not necessarily OE has been the criterion for inclusion of CPs, whatever the meaning of the verb: the occurrence of a verb such as *love*, which is semantically different from the meaning of *make love*, was not a determining criterion for exclusion of the CP formed with *love*. In the second case, however, there are verbs such as *do a robbery*, as in (14), which includes a noun that is etymologically linked to the simple verb *rob*. To identify members of CPs following the first criterion I made use of the *OED* and checked all nouns one by one.

(14) I was sent for to know if I could see any thing of the people that **did this robbery**. (1750s)
(15) Gif ðu hine forgitst, hit **hearmaðþe** sylfum and na Gode. (*OED* – Ælfric, Homilies vol. I. 140)

Based on the mentioned criteria, combinations including *take business* and *have difficulty* have been excluded from the group of CPs because there are no corresponding simple verbs and nor are they derivative of other simplexes.

1.5.2 Concordance-based analysis of selected CPs

CPs have been retrieved by using the concordancer WordSmith Tools 6.0 (Scott 2013), which comprises n-grams of up to 6 words and allows visualization of the traditional vertical layout of the concordancer. WordSmith Tools 6.0 includes Concord, which visualizes concordance lines within a selected span of the context to both right and left. The window was set at +5 to the left and +5 to the right, and this allows visualization of CPs and any intervening elements, such as adverbs and adjectives. As suggested, the focus has been on CPs formed with *do*, *give*, *have*, *make*, and *take*. I made use of single types for each of the mentioned verbs and identified all nominal components selecting instances of CPs that respected well-defined linguistic criteria (§1.5.1).

1.5.3 Quantitative analysis

To provide a quantitative description of CPs, I calculated the raw frequency (Rf), the normalized frequency (Nf), and percentages. Moreover, different rates have often been compared and the difference is expressed in terms of a percentage (Diff%). The description has been complemented with the calculation of the type/token ratio (TTR), the log-likelihood (LL) score and logistic regression. TTR is a useful measure to identify the degree of productivity of each basis (Torre Alonso et al. 2014) and may reveal the ability of a basis to form other CPs. LL[4] calculates the statistical significance of differences between values in two corpora (Rayson et al. 2004; Brezina 2018) whereas logistic regression[5] estimates the effect of the variable time on the distribution of CPs over time, and this includes statistical significance information (Brezina 2018).

1.6 The structure of the book

This monograph is organized into six chapters. Chapter 2 focuses on the literature on CPs. Specifically, existing studies have been grouped according to the period they examine to provide an overview of the linguistic evolution of CPs since their beginning. This approach allows the evaluation of processes of change characterizing CPs from OE to Present Day English (PDE), and the contextualization of the results within the histories of CPs of other periods.

Chapter 3 describes the linguistic features of CPs during the LModE period. It includes a description of the frequency of CPs and the productivity of the bases *do*, *give*, *have*, *make*, and *take*.

Chapter 4 describes the syntactic and semantic features of CPs across the years 1750–1850. Chapter 5 examines the processes of change characterizing CPs, which include grammaticalization, lexicalization, idiomatization, direct formation, and analogy. The aim is to test whether and the extent to which these verbs were affected by similar paths of development that characterized other multi-word verbs of the LModE time as examined in other works (Rodríguez-Puente 2016, 2019; Leone 2019, 2023).

Chapter 6 is devoted to conclusions and suggests future paths of research.

Notes

1 The brackets specify the date when the example reported was used. All examples reported in the present chapter are retrieved from the *Late Modern English - Old Bailey Corpus* covering the years 1750–1850 and including recordings of speech held at the Old Bailey, London's Central Criminal Court.
2 A selection of the proceedings also forms the basis of the *Old Bailey Corpus* (*OBC*) covering the years 1720–1913 (Huber et al. 2016). I decided not to use the *OBC* because the aim is to compare the results obtained with other studies on LModE undertaken on the *LModE-OBC* by Leone (2021, 2022, 2023) examining phrasal verbs and the development of other multi-word

verbs such as prepositional verbs, phrasal-prepositional verbs, and verb-adjective combinations.
3 The *ARCHER* corpus is accessible on the CQPweb server (Corpus Query Processor), which is a database created and managed by Lancaster University (Hardie 2012).
4 The LL score has been calculated with the LL calculator and effect size (Rayson & Garside 2000; Rayson 2008), available at https://ucrel.lancs.ac.uk/llwizard.html.
5 Logistic regression has been calculated with Python, which is a programming language useful for linguistic analysis and quantitative description.

2 History

2.1 Old English and Middle English: the establishment of composite predicates

Knowledge of CPs in the OE period is rather fragmentary and mostly based on a few CPs taken as case studies. This tendency arises from the difficulties in classifying CPs from early times because these verbs, especially in early times, occur with the status of collocations, that is, free combinations rather than single lexemes. This is the case with Mitchell's (1985) work, which does not mention verbs that form collocations with specific nominal elements, and Mitchell and Robinson's (1992) study that provides a comprehensive account of OE without, however, examining aspects concerning the collocational value of light verbs and their ability to select specific nominal elements. According to Akimoto and Brinton (1999: 22–23), two major problems have partly discouraged investigations of CPs: (i) "whether the pattern of Old English N + V corresponding to the modern composite predicate has a semantic relationship to the corresponding single verb," as would be the case of *have a look* and *look*; (ii) "how we should decide the semantic 'lightness' of the Old English verb and the semantic 'heaviness' of the Old English to 'noun of action' or 'deverbal nominal'."

CPs are first attested in OE when there are nominalized expressions such as *gewin drugon*, "they fought," and *fyl geniman*, "take a fall, be killed," which are characterized by the semantic prominence of the noun (Klaeber 1943, discussed in Claridge 2000). CPs are used in a very limited way, when compared with the following periods, since they gradually become more popular in ME (Hiltunen 1983), undergoing significant development during the modern English times (Akimoto & Brinton 1999: 21; see Görlach 1991). Visser (1963) mentions some CPs formed with *habban* and *niman* used in OE, but his work is limited in some respects: indeed, as Claridge (2000: 94) notes, he does not account for the frequency of use of instances, and he does not specify "whether they are phrasal units in the sense the modern types are."

A more detailed description of CPs in OE is provided by Akimoto and Brinton (1999) who examine various dictionaries, including the *Dictionary of Old English* and the *Middle English Dictionary* (*MED*), and these give empirical evidence of the linguistic status of these verbs in early times. They note that changes in the word order and vocabulary are the factors that mostly influenced the use of CPs in OE, along with cases of rivalry: there is linguistic competition among alternative base verbs, but also between CPs and simplex verbs. First, *sellan* and *giefan*, *don* and *macian*, and *niman* and *tacan*, are often set in paradigmatic competition. At the same time, there are cases of interchangeability of verbal forms such as *don*, *niman*, or *habban* when used in combination with a single noun such as *weg*. Second, there are some CPs and simplexes that are linked by a relation of synonymy, and others that are not, as in the case of *loc macian*, "make an agreement," which is to some extent different from *lucan* "to conclude" (Akimoto & Brinton 1999). The examination of data reveals that there are 114 different CPs, which are formed with 5 bases and 86 nouns working as their collocates, such as *andan habban* "have envy," *geleafan habban* "have faith," *hweowe habban* "have sorrow," *geleafan niman* "believe," *fultum sellan* "give help," *hyge sellan* "give one's hearth /mind" (Akimoto & Brinton 1999: 21–55). According to Brinton and Akimoto (1999), the verb *(ge)don* decreases in use due to its competition with the verb *(ge)macian* (i.e. the modern "make") in consequence of processes of borrowing from French that limited its use in combination with nouns working as the semantic focus of the combination. A partially similar history characterizes *sellan* (i.e. the modern "give"), which started to compete with *giefan* and was replaced by it. These examples prove that the history of single CPs was influenced by the occurrence of alternative forms and that there were interference phenomena in the English verb system that worked variously on CPs. Linguistically, Akimoto and Brinton (1999) highlight that in OE CPs preserved the status of collocations and were not

16 *History*

completely grammaticalized and lexicalized as single units. Moreover, existing combinations did not show "such systematic idiomatization as its Modern English development" (Akimoto & Brinton 1999: 53), and on many occasions, it is even impossible to determine whether they exhibited an aspectual connotation, as would be the case with some deverbal nouns in PDE (Brinton & Akimoto 1999: 6). CPs may even express duration (Wierzbicka 1982) and perfectivity (Stein 1991), that is, they may express the viewpoint of speakers on the action and the temporal qualities of the situation expressed by the verb (Brinton 1988).

During the ME period, CPs became more frequent. Examination of Chaucer's and Malory's works, and CPs included in the *MED* undertaken by Matsumoto (1999), reveals that CPs were increasingly used and that they even started to work as stylistic devices which were the preferred form in prose on many occasions. This scholar finds 900 different types of CPs, which is a high number if compared with those of the previous period, meaning that CPs were affected by increasing productivity. Similar to PDE, CPs of ME occur in two patterns: (i) V + N pattern, for example, *maken faith* "to give assurance, pledge one's word" (*MED – OED*, quoted in Matsumoto 1999: 62); (ii) V + N + P pattern, such as *maken an ende of* "to finish or conclude (a speech, story, etc.)" (*MED*, quoted in Matsumoto 1999: 63). The existence of these two patterns corroborates the hypothesis whereby CPs in ME started to exhibit features that they still have in PDE (Visser 1963), such as the ability to occur both with and without a preposition.

Similar considerations emerge from the study of *The Paston Letters* carried out by Tanabe (1999) who emphasizes that CPs of ME can vary in their internal constituency and occur both with and without a preposition. The most frequent base verbs which can be observed in *The Paston Letters* are *do*, *give*, *have*, *make*, and *take*, which reach a frequency of 509 occurrences and behave in a similar way to their modern counterpart, that is, they allow   nominal modifiers such as *many*, *more*, *much*, and *such* (Tanabe 1999: 115), as in (1), or adjectives, as in (2)-(4):[1]

(1) for I trust to **haue more joye** of hym þan I haue of them
...[MP 220: 11–12]
"for I trust to have more joy from him than I have from them"
(2) and that shold be to hem **the grettyst confort that thay myȝt haue**. [MP 184: 18–19]

"and that should be to them the greatest comfort that they could have"
(3) she **made hym gentil chere** in gyntyl wyse [AP 13: 5–6]
"She made him gentle cheer (entertained him well) in a courteous manner"
(4) if he **have redy help**; [MP 144: 13]
"if he has ready help"

ME is also the period when CPs started to show variation in the use of the article, and to occur with both a definite or indefinite article, or zero articles, as would be the case with *give answere*, and *give an answere*, or also *make excuce*, *make an end* and *make a returne* (Tanabe 1999: 117). A peculiar feature of CPs in ME is that, in most cases, they do not passivize because of their status as "highly fixed idioms" (Tanabe 1999: 120) and passivization is obtained with *there*-constructions, as in (5):[2]

(5) and there **was made appoyntment** be-twen hem by the aduyce of bothe there conceylis [MP 177: 6–7]
"and there was made appointment between them, by the advice of both their counsels"

The only case that allows passivization in Tanabe's (1999: 120; see Matsumoto 2005) work is *take an action* which is "an exception for this tendency." The internal and limited use of CPs in their passive forms also emerges from studies undertaken by Moralejo Gárate (2002) and Sánchez Roura (2003). Specifically, they draw attention to their admission of modification, complementation, and determination possibilities (Moralejo Gárate 2002: 185) and that the "lack of passivization suggests general fixity of the structure" (Sánchez Roura 2003: 197).

An innovative aspect of ME is that there is an increasing number of CPs that occur with an idiomatic meaning. Specifically, Matsumoto (1999: 89, 91) observes that there are CPs that involve body nouns like *haven herte* "to have the heart (to do …), bear (to do …), have a desire (to do …)," or *haven tonge* "to be able to speak; have a tongue (able to say …)," or also *maken a face* "to make, or put in an appearance." There are also other figurative uses, as in the case of *make marchaudie of* "take advantage of (…) exploit" or *maken leve* "to abandon (…) quit" (Matsumoto 1999: 92), which indicate ongoing processes of idiomatization. This entails that, in many respects, in ME CPs are very close in use to that of PDE but distant from their use in OE: for example, *take/have* + noun combinations mark the state vs. event distinction that they still have in PDE, and exhibit features that also other multi-word verbs such as phrasal verbs from ME to PDE have (Matsumoto 2007).

2.2 Early Modern English: the spread of composite predicates

CPs of EModE have received limited attention in comparison with early periods because of the close link between EModE and ModE (Hiltunen 1999: 138). Interest in CPs of the EModE period is attested in Visser's work (1963), which gives a detailed description of the processes of change affecting these verbs that combine with stable features: in this regard, he mentions verbs such as *have a mind*, and *catch hold of*, proving that CPs of the time were already acquiring the linguistic forms that exist in PDE. Other works examining CPs of the EModE time include those of Koskenniemi (1977), Kytö (1999), Hiltunen (1999), and Claridge (2000). Specifically, Koskenniemi (1977) works on texts written during the English Renaissance and on Shakespeare's dramas, investigating the frequency and linguistic features of CPs for the years 1550–1590. She further enhances the close link between EModE and PDE but also demonstrates that they increase their popularity as a result of contact with other languages such as Latin and French. These two languages hugely affected the history of English in its early stages (Mugglestone 2006; Trudgill 2016; Lavidas & Bergs 2020) and also favored the establishment of new CPs that emerged as translations of Romance equivalent verbs in EModE (Koskenniemi 1977).

The theoretical status of CPs over time is the focus of the work of Hiltunen (1999) who describes them as idiomatic expressions that emerged as an effect of the analytic drift which was operative from early times in English. He examines a corpus of more than one million words, which includes poems and plays written around 1600. It is stored electronically in the *Oxford Text Archive* (*OTA*), and he notices that, despite many changes having already taken place by the beginning of the EModE time, these verbs "undergo significant developments in several respects" (Hiltunen 1999: 133). During the EModE period, indeed, the CPs *do*, *give*, *make*, *take* established themselves as verbs showing internal variation and occurrence in four

History   19

patterns: (i) verb + *a / an* + (modifier / s) + noun, for example, *make an end*, *have a shrewd gesse*; (ii) verb + (modifier / s) + noun, for example, *give order*, *make returne*; (iii) verb + *the* + (modifier / s) + noun, for example, *make a full show*; (iv) verb + (*the*) + (modifier / s) + noun plural, for example, *make amends*. The most frequent base verbs are *have* and *make*, which combine with diverse nouns to form CPs. On many occasions, they develop also as idiomatic expressions, despite most of the CPs remaining literal in meaning in EModE.

An approach based on the collocational profile of CPs formed with *do, give, have, make*, and take characterizes Kytö's (1999) work, which queries the Early Modern section of the *Helsinki Corpus of English Texts* and a total of 551,000 words to identify the degree of productivity and variation of the lexical profile of these verbs over the years 1500–1710. As with Hiltunen's work, the most frequent verb is *make*, and it is also the most productive verb: the TTR, which "reflects the use of a varied vocabulary in the texts" (Kytö 1999: 171) is constant with the verbs *make* (0.36), *have* (0.36), *give* (0.34), and more limited in the case of *take* (0.24) and *do* (0.26). Each of these verbs also presents similar levels of frequency over time with a more marked difference between the uses of *give* and *do* in 1500 and 1710, exhibiting an increasing and a decreasing trend respectively. Moreover, these bases show some collocational preferences and a tendency to occur with specific nominal parts, and this emphasizes their unitary status since EModE. For example, Kytö (1999: 177) reports on *make act / complaint / discovery / answer / trial, have care / meeting, make end, do sermon, give account*, and notes the absence of register-based differences in their use; Moreover, she finds that CPs occur both in "more informal and personal writing" such as private correspondence, and also in more formal texts such as legal texts (Kytö 1999: 178).

A more recent study on EModE is one undertaken by Claridge (2000), who examines the *Lampeter Corpus* (Siemund & Claridge 1997), which is a multi-genre corpus including both written and spoken data (in the form of speech-based texts), describing CPs between the years 1640 and 1740. She divides verbo-nominal combinations into three groups (Claridge 2000: 40): (i) simple verb-noun unit, for example, *take a walk*, (ii) verb-noun-preposition unit, *catch sight of*; (iii) verb-prepositional phrase unit, for example, *put in execution*, and investigates both the overall trend of CPs and the features of each group. It is interesting to note that Claridge's classification is broader than any other, as the inclusion of a verb such as *take into consideration* and *pay attention to* reveals the intention to extend analysis also to base verbs that are not immediately followed by the nominal part, as well as to CPs that do not include light verbs as their bases. This is not the approach adopted in the present work, which is exclusively based on combinations formed by the light verbs *do*, *give*, *have*, *make*, and *take* complemented by a noun, and the reason lies in the fact that the study focuses on CPs intended as verb-nominal combinations in a narrow sense, that is, on light verbs immediately followed by a noun working as the semantic focus of the combination. The inclusion of CPs formed by a base verb immediately followed by a preposition is, in the present work, seen as a subtype of CPs, which should be treated separately given its diverse morphological structure. The examination of CPs reveals that a line of continuity can be observed with more modern times, and this is corroborated by consideration of the status of the bases *to be* and *to have* that mostly occur in the pattern verb + noun + preposition as reported in modern grammars (Biber et al. 1999, 2021).

The examination of the path CPs followed from OE to LModE is the main objective of Brinton's (1999) work that describes the linguistic features of these verbs and the factors promoting their renewal. Specifically, she attributes a major role in the history of CPs to the influence of other languages, word-formation processes and the tendency towards analyticity. The relative stability CPs bear in EModE anticipates their tendency towards conventionalization, which is more prominent in the following LModE when they increase their frequency of use (Brinton 2008).

A very recent study on CPs of the EModE time, which can be considered comparatively in the present research, is Wang's (2019) contribution on CPs during the years 1560–1760. The reasons why this study is particularly relevant for the present research are twofold: (i) it has been undertaken on the *Corpus of English Dialogues*, and specifically on speech-related texts (drama and trials); (ii) it covers the years 1560–1760. This creates a line of continuity between his findings and those presented in the present study because of the focus on speech-related texts, and of the period which ends in the year immediately preceding those covered in the *LModE-OBC* (1750–1850). Wang's (2019) work describes the frequency, lexical productivity and syntactic features of the verbs *do*, *have*, *give*, *make*, and *take*, proving that *do/take* + noun combinations are mostly affected by lexicalization and are less productive, whereas *give/have/make* combinations are grammaticalized instances that exhibit specific collocational preferences.

2.3 Late Modern English: stability and change

During the LModE period, CPs have been treated as combinations that emerged as a result of interacting factors promoting the increase in analyticity: "English changed from a **synthetic**[3] language, with many endings on nouns and verbs indicating grammatical functions such as subject and object, to a mostly **analytic** language with almost no endings" (van Gelderen 2006: 23) while developing periphrastic structures like CPs (Brinton 1996).

The establishment of CPs and processes of change are the core arguments of studies undertaken by Akimoto (1999) and Brinton (1999) who published their findings in a book devoted to collocational and idiomatic aspects of composite predicates in the history of English. To prove the existence of ongoing changes affecting CPs of the eighteenth and nineteenth centuries, Akimoto (1999) queries a corpus including many different text types and the *Oxford English Dictionary*, which allows the collection of examples from a variety of genres such as fiction, essays, letters, and drama. She examines the bases *do, give, have, make,* and *take* when followed by a deverbal noun and identifies the most common collocations for each of them. For example, she reports that *do* collocates with *justice, honour, harm, work, duty,* whereas *account, leave, pleasure, reason, trouble* are preferred by the verb *give,* as in (6)–(7):[4]

(6) but people that will **do their duty**, must have some trouble (Richardson: 164).
(7) Without waiting for your answer to my last, I proceed to **give you an account of** your journey to London (Smollett: 79).

At the same time, Akimoto (1999) notices that a noun can occur in combination with various bases without significant change in meaning, as in the case of *do credit* and *give credit,* as in (8)–(9).[5] This corroborates the link between LModE and OE when cases of interchangeability of verbal forms are first attested (Akimoto & Brinton 1999).

(8) and assigning for it sundry reasons physical and moral which **did more credit** to her person than her modesty (Letters [Haydon]: 227).
(9) but it is stranger that some of his friends should **have given credit** to his groundless opinion (Boswell: 49).

Examination of the examples Akimoto (1999) provides, on balance, the hypothesis formulated by Claridge (2000) stating that most of the changes were over by the end of the EModE period, which, nonetheless, does not preclude further more limited signs of innovation. An important factor in the LModE period is that there is "a remarkable tendency in the process of idiomatization" (Akimoto 1999: 225) which affects instances of CPs consequently moving from concreteness to abstractness and developing new more opaque connotations. In this respect, Akimoto (1999) identifies cases of idiomatization affecting instances that were previously involved in reanalysis. Idiomatization is conceptualized as a gradual process by Akimoto (1989) characterized by four steps. Taking *lose sight of* as a case study, it is possible to represent the four steps as follows (Akimoto 1989: 354–358):

1. All constituents have an unbounded status
2. The verb and the following noun become fixed; often also the preposition is stabilized
3. The constituents undergo reanalysis, for example, from [lose] [sight of NP] to [lose sight of] [NP]
4. The already formed lexeme may undergo idiomatization

According to Akimoto, during the EModE period most of the CPs were at stage 3 and started to occur as multi-word combinations, entering into stage 4 in the following LModE period. Moreover, during the LModE period, CPs started to vary their nominal elements and to occur with nominal derived from a phrasal verb (Brinton 1999: 256), that is, with nouns that emerged as zero-derived forms from the corresponding phrasal verbs, for example, *clean-up* (N) from *to clean up* (V). Another peculiar aspect of this period is that emphasized by Matsumoto (2008: 149), stating that many CPs occur with body nouns: *change hands*, *lay one's fingers*, *rib skins*. The increasing use of nominal parts belonging to this semantic field was accompanied by increasing idiomaticity of combinations, which were also featured with metaphorical interpretation: this is, for example, the

History 23

case of *wring one's hand* used with the meaning of "worry," but then substituted by "meaningful gestures" (Matsumoto 2008: 157).

2.4 Present Day English: current forms and uses

CPs have been described in many grammars written by Poutsma (1926), Curme (1931), and Kruisinga (1931), who are especially interested in defining the linguistic features, the single components of the combinations and their lexeme status. Specifically, Poutsma (1926) examines the base verbs and attributes to them the purpose of a connective, which is a hypothesis confirmed by the presence of nouns in combination with various bases that carry minimal or no difference in meaning, for example, *make a call* or *give a call*. Aspects concerning the morphological origin of CPs are the core arguments of Kruisinga's (1931) work, which defines the nominal part of CPs as "converted" nouns that are isomorphic forms of other simple verbs, that is, linked derivationally to simplexes. The function attributed to the base verb is also discussed in Curme (1931), describing CPs as verbs that are very similar to the copula *to be* whose function is to link the predicate noun to its subject."

These works have heavily influenced the following studies on CPs and inform modern conceptualizations such as those undertaken by Live (1973), Bolinger (1971), and Fraser (1976). A more recent work is Cattell's (1984), which represents one of the most detailed examinations of CPs and their use in PDE. In Cattell's (1984: 2) view, the verbs *make, give, have, take*, and *do* "seem semantically very 'light'," whereas the meaning is embedded in the nominal part, which is a typical aspect of CPs since their emergence. In recent times, CPs have been treated as verbs that include an eventive object (Quirk et al. 1985) and described as members of multi-word verbs along with phrasal verbs, prepositional verbs, and other multi-word verb combinations (Biber et al. 1999, 2021). As expected, in their examination of CPs, a descriptive view is taken by these grammars. CPs are characterized by specific functionalities, including dynamic uses of *have*, which can have meanings that go beyond the stative use of "to possess," state vs event contrast, and phraseological variability with nouns collocating with diverse bases with no change in meaning, for example, *give attention / pay attention*. CPs have been the subject of investigation in studies following diverse theoretical perspectives and treated as examples of multiple inheritance and constructional change within a Construction Grammar framework (Trousdale 2008), or examined as phraseological forms standing "where grammar and lexis meet" (Brinton 2008: 33).

Notes

1 Examples taken from Tanabe (1999: 115, 106). MP stands for Margaret Paston; the number in parenthesis refers to letter number and line number of Davis' edition (Tanabe 1999: 131, note 5).
2 Example taken from Tanabe (1999: 120).
3 Bold in original.
4 Examples taken from Akimoto (1999: 209, 208).
5 Examples taken from Akimoto (1999: 208, 210).

3 Linguistic features

3.1 Distribution of composite predicates

CPs are often been treated as verbs characterized by a limited frequency of use up to the EModE period when they started to increase in popularity, becoming one of the segmentalized structures that feature the English verb system along with other multi-word verbs like phrasal verbs, verb-adjective combinations, and verb-verb combinations (Hiltunen 1983; Brinton 1996; Tanabe 1999; Claridge 2000). Indeed, CPs were relatively frequent in early times, as suggested by Claridge (2000) who proves that CPs of the years 1640–1740 – which are named verbo-nominal combinations – show increasing use: they are attested at a rate of 1,994, that is, 1.7 Nf per 1,000 words.

The examination of CPs occurring in the *LModE-OBC* reveals that CPs overall occur at 3,044 hits, that is, 3.01 Nf per 1,000 words, which means that the LMod period is characterized by increasing use if compared with the rates attested in the years examined by Claridge (2000). There are two major components to consider to evaluating divergences between these two periods: (i) the *LModE-OBC* includes speech-based genres of trials and witness testimonies only, which means that the language is close to spoken colloquial data (Huber 2007; Culpeper & Kytö 2010); (ii) there can be decades showing an extensive use of CPs which could render the results biased.

In the first case, the rates calculated in the years 1750–1850 are double in comparison with those obtained in EModE, as reported by Claridge (2000), which corroborates the hypothesis that, in addition to internal mechanisms of change that may favor the use of CPs in LModE, there can be divergences linked to the text types and the degree of formality. If accepted, this assertion has two

DOI: 10.4324/9781003410256-3

consequences: (i) it could implicate that CPs are close to other multi-word verbs, including phrasal verbs that are typically associated with spoken data (Thim 2012; Rodríguez-Puente 2016); (ii) it entails that CPs are used in colloquial language.

As for the first point, the high rates of CPs in the *LModE-OBC* are in line with what has already been proven by Leone (2023) who investigates the development of phrasal verbs, prepositional verbs, and phrasal-prepositional verbs highlighting that these multi-word verbs are more frequent in spoken data than written data. On that occasion, she compares the use of these verbs with those reported in Claridge's (2000) work and attributes a prominent role to the medium to explain the divergences observed: despite the use of *formulae* and conventions linked to the courtroom, trials are proxies to spoken language (Culpeper & Kytö 2010), whereas the *Lampeter Corpus* includes both written and spoken language, which could suggest that phrasal verbs are more frequently used in spoken language. Acceptance of this hypothesis implies that CPs exhibit a linguistic behavior that is similar to that of other multi-word verbs also for what concerns the medium and colloquiality. Examination of phrasal verbs over the years 1620–1760 undertaken by Rodríguez-Puente and Obaya Cueli (2022: 827) has demonstrated that they "were well entrenched in the spoken, colloquial language of the EModE period" and that "growth of phrasal verbs is particularly marked in those registers which most closely represent the spoken language of the past, namely trial proceedings and witness depositions." Likewise, it is possible to suppose that one of the reasons explaining the divergent rates observed between EModE and LModE is the degree of colloquiality of the texts, which grants CPs the status of verbs that are especially used in colloquial language also in LModE. The examination of register differences falls outside the scope of the present study but critical evaluation of existing studies on multi-word verbs may support this hypothesis, which is further corroborated by findings concerning CPs of early periods. The examination of CPs as verbs that are signs of colloquiality is the aim of Sánchez Routa (2003: 197) who studies the *Wakefield Plays* and states that "the fact that so many idioms [CPs] appear in the data helps us further support the claim that such texts are, in fact, colloquial in nature."

Moving on to the second factor identified above, to guarantee that the rates reflect the real use of CPs and that one or more decades using extensively specific CPs do not affect the results, it is necessary to go beyond simple counts and measure the distributional properties of these verbs over the decades. The calculation of the rates across the decades may help the identification of further aspects explaining the divergences observed in EModE and LModE. Language always changes, new structures can expand their use or may undergo retraction, and some temporal windows may have a much bigger impact on the overall count, revealing signs of variation and change. To evaluate the extent to which CPs modified their frequency of use over time, and identify ongoing processes of change, the rates per decade, as shown in Figure 3.1, were calculated.

CPs show a relatively stable trend with a steady decline up to the 1810s, which are the years that reach the lowest rate of 2.21. Expressed in terms of Diff% , the 1810s are –26.22% (LL 24.02, significant at p<0.01) if compared with the rate of the 1790s, and –35.97 % (LL 55.40, significant at p<0.01) if compared with the following 1830s. Beyond this declining trend, however, paradoxically there is proof of increasing use when comparing the rates of the 1750s and 1830s, that is, CPs shift from Nf 3.21 to 3.45 respectively: the 1750s are –6.93 (LL 1.73) but these results are not significant statistically at p<0.01. Overall, examination of differences among the decades reveals that all decades show variation and that they all contribute to the overall results equally. CPs are far from being stable, which means that there

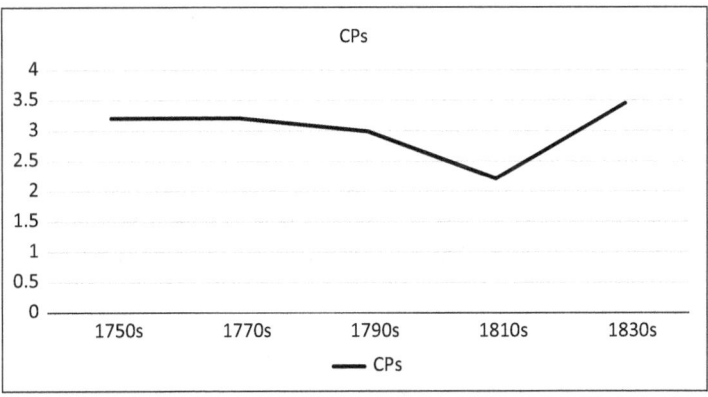

Figure 3.1 Composite predicates over the years 1750–1850 (Nf per 1,000 words).

28 *Linguistic features*

may be ongoing processes of innovation qualifying the LModE time as a period still characterized by change. These considerations support the hypothesis whereby there are also processes of renewal that influence the rates of CPs in LModE, which do not relate to the nature of the text types, partly explaining the divergences between EModE and LModE discussed above.

To examine the correlation between the variable time and the frequency of CPs over the years, I studied lexico-grammatical variation with the statistical technique often used in diachronic studies, that is, logistic regression. Linear modeling is an effective measure when the aim is to depict a picture of instances like CPs and their frequency over time and is preferable to mixed-effect modeling based on the variation within single samples, which is, instead, useful to focus on single texts or speakers. Mixed-effect modeling may, indeed, unlock internal variation within the texts, but it does not give access to tendencies, as is the case of the development of specific structures like CPs that are under investigation in the present study. Figure 3.2 represents the graph obtained for linear regression calculated on CPs over time.

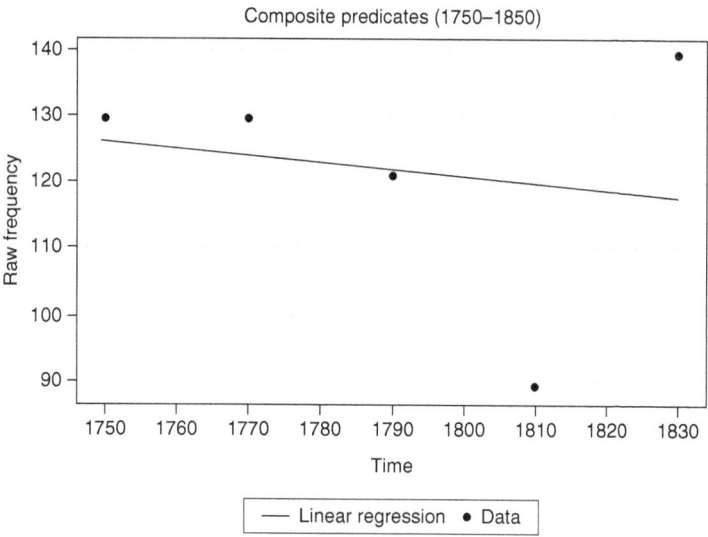

Figure 3.2 Linear regression over the years 1750–1850.

As shown in Figure 3.2, CPs are still characterized by variation over time; However, the change is not statistically significant ($R^2 = 0.02894238282295262$). The results obtained are not surprising since the LModE period is often depicted as a time characterized by signs of stability and more proxy to PDE than any other period (Hundt 2014). Moreover, the rates of selected light verbs may also be influenced by the idiolect of one or more speakers extensively using CPs, or by the recurrent use of CPs formed with one single basis showing a higher degree of flexibility which overall contributes to the final rate in each decade. This highlights the need to calculate the rates of each base verb and to describe their linguistic behavior over time, which is the topic of the next section.

Identifying the factors rendering CPs popular over the years is difficult, but it is possible to formulate hypotheses based on insightful discussions made by other scholars examining the growth of analytic structures like CPs. The reference here is to van Gelderen's (2018: ix) work investigating changes with causatives and noticing that the light verbs were used to make the structure more obvious.

The history of English also shows a typological change that makes the picture more complex: there is an increase in analytic marking and a decrease as well as an increase in synthetic marking. Certain parts of the English language have become more analytic through the increased use of light verbs, such as *make*, *do*, *put*, and *get*, and particles showing results. As for synthetic, there has been a loss of transitivizing and causticizing affixes but also an increase in synthetic marking because labile verbs can be seen as more synthetic.

It should be hypothesized that there is a combination of linguistic issues that have promoted the increasing use of CPs in LModE as well as in early times, such as "the frequent strengthening of the old meaning by a causative light verb and the use of a reflexive with the new meaning," which are discussed by van Gelderen (2018: 174) in her work on the diachrony of verb meaning. Considerations provided by this scholar may find application in the case of CPs of LModE. She states that "these additions [new instances] provide evidence of a change: because the inner aspect becomes ambiguous, light verbs, telic adverbs, and reflexives clarify a sentence's aspect" (van Gelderen 2018: 174). These are processes that are not observable in

30 *Linguistic features*

the *LModE-OBC* but that may have played a role also in the widespread use of CPs in the years 1750–1850.

3.2 The base verbs

Observation of the trend of each base verb shown in Figure 3.3 reveals that, as already hypothesized, some bases occur more frequently than others to form CPs in the data, and that there is an unstable trend.

Overall, *give*, *have*, and *make* are the most popular CPs, which occupy 24.5%, 29.92%, and 24.40% of all occurrences respectively, whereas *take* and *do* represent 17.50% and 3.61%.

The results obtained partly overlap with those reported in Wang's (2019: 30) work highlighting that in EModE, *have* "constituted a major part of CPs" in trials whereas "*do* appeared to be the least productive." Differently, Claridge (2000) states that *make* is the most common basis in EModE which raises questions concerning the reasons beyond this kind of discrepancy. An immediate explanation could lie in the text type again. Wang queries the *Corpus of English Dialogues* (*CED*) including speech-based genres whereas Claridge's dataset includes both written and spoken genres. Acceptance of this hypothesis is, however, open to debate if considering works on CPs of previous times based on written texts, like Tanabe's (1999) work. Specifically, examination of the data reported in Tanabe's (1999) study on ME reveals that *have* is the most common basis, meaning that the results obtained in LModE are in line with the linguistic behavior of

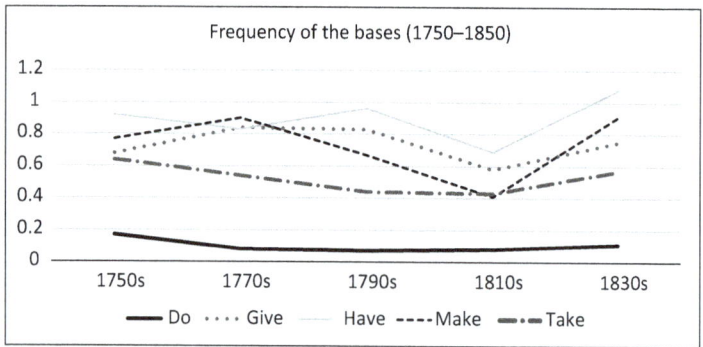

Figure 3.3 Light verbs over the years 1750–1850 (Nf per 1,000 words).

these bases in earlier times. This strengthens the role of medium in the linguistic choice of CPs based on light verbs, and grants Claridge's ranking a particularly important function: there is a break in the use of bases, which may be related to text types but not solely. Acceptance of this assertion does not imply the absence of other influencing factors. In this regard, it should be hypothesized that, given the diachronic view of the present study, issues like diverse degrees of productivity of bases, which is an effective measure to understand the degree of innovativeness of CPs, may also explain divergences. Moreover, the existence of variation in the use of the bases *do*, *give*, *have*, *make*, and *take* could ideally be due to linguistic variability characterizing each of them: often, indeed, frequency of use and involvement in language change are closely linked to each other. This reminds us of the need for consideration of the lexico-grammatical features of CPs, and variation in their constituents, as will be described in the next paragraphs. As Brinton (2008: 37) notes, many components may limit comparative analysis: "varied types of corpora used, different morphosyntactic and semantic definitions of the composite predicate." However, the limits may be overcome by considering all factors – both linguistic and external – which can explain variation and change.

3.3 Phrasal profile and productivity of composite predicates

3.3.1 Phraseological variation across the years 1750–1850

The definition of CPs as combinations formed by a light verb, that is, *do*, *give*, *have*, *make*, and *take*, followed by a deverbal noun conveying most of the meaning, implies that the combinations allow internal variability. Indeed, while light verbs are a well-defined class, the nominal component is extremely variable, which justifies the treatment of CPs as phraseological forms that stand between grammar and lexis: (i) they are syntactically complex combinations formed by V + N, which is often preceded by a determiner (e.g. *a/an/the*), and sometimes followed by a preposition, as in (1); (ii) they form a single unit that often has idiomatic meaning, as in (2):

(1) he said he could **give a good account of** himself. (1750s)
(2) I did not hear him **make the noise**. (1810s)

The nominal component of CPs occurring in the data always consists of abstract nouns that are etymologically related to the verbal stem (*make a speech/speak*) or linguistically related to it (*have access/ access*), working as the semantic center of the combinations (Algeo 1995). Moreover, CPs allow internal modification. On the one hand, the V + N is not fossilized as an invariable string and may permit intervening objects, like adverbs and adjectives, as in (3), in addition to being used without any intervening element, as in (4). On the other hand, there can be instances institutionalized as single fixed combinations that are often non-compositional in meaning. All instances may stand in paradigmatic competition with simple verbs (Brinton 1996; Biber et al. 1999, 2021) as is the case of *give information* and *inform*, as in (5)–(6):

(3) they all **gave a different account of** their coming there. (1750s)
(4) I **made enquiry** of the next door neighbour (1770s)

(5) and I can **give information** where the seals were disposed of. (1810s)
(6) I thought it not prudent **to inform** him. (1750s)

The idea whereby CPs are multi-word units characterized by internal modification, variability in the constituents and often idiomatic meaning has been defended by many scholars highlighting the various nouns each of the light verb can combine with (Akimoto 1989, 1999; Traugott 1999; Claridge 2000).

Do collocates frequently with nouns like *job*, *harm*, *injury*, *robbery*, and *work*, as shown in (7), whereas *give* is often followed by *account*, *alarm*, *answer*, *charge*, *direction*, and *information*, as seen in (8). *Have* is often followed by *doubt*, *conversation*, *information*, *reason*, and *suspicion*, as in (9), whereas *make* collocates with *answer*, *assault*, *complaint*, *noise*, and *promise*, as shown in (10). Differently from these verbs, *take* is used with a limited number of nouns like *account*, *care*, *hold*, and *notice*, as in (11):

(7) he wanted the young man **to do a private job** for him (1750s)
(8) he **gave her some surly answer**. (1770s)
(9) if she had been so indicted, you would **have had no doubt of** convicting her (1770s)

(10) The deceased **made a noise** with his throat, as if he could not speak. (1810s)
(11) I can tell by the handkerchief, I **took notice of** the border of the handkerchief at the time it was open. (1770s)

Some of the deverbal nouns for each light verb are included in Table 3.1.

Beyond the ability of a base verb to combine with various nouns to form literal, semi-compositional, or even idiomatic units, there are, however, some preferences, and this also happens in LModE, as shown in Table 3.2 reporting the three most frequent CPs in the LModE.

All bases combine with nominal components that belong to various semantic categories. For example, considering some of the categories identified by Moralejo (2000) the nouns may express feelings (*care*), offensive actions (*robbery*), mental actions (*doubt*), speech (*answer*),

Table 3.1 Some nouns occurring in composite predicates

do	job, harm, injury, robbery, work
give	account, alarm, answer, blow, character, charge, credit, direction, description, evidence, information, notice, opinion, order, possession, price, reason, reference, suspicion, warning
have	access, advice, appearance, acquaintance, charge, conversation, custody, deal, dealing, discourse, information, intention, knowledge, mind, objection, occasion, reason, pleasure, quarrel, satisfaction,
make	agreement, assault, complaint, confession, discovery, doubt, enquiry, escape, excuse, haste, impression, noise, observation, promise, reply, satisfaction
take	account, advantage, breakfast, care, charge, effect, hold, measure, notice, walk

Table 3.2 Top composite predicates of each base verb: Raw frequency

do	give	have	make	take
work (25)	character (143)	doubt (94)	assault (94)	care (132)
harm (22)	account (95)	hold (69)	answer (55)	notice (101)
job (14)	information (94)	conversation (67)	noise (44)	hold (99)

34 *Linguistic features*

motion (*direction*), agreement (*agreement*), homage (*honour*). However, once again, there can be some preferences: while the nominal parts of most frequent CPs formed with *do*, *give*, and *take* belong to various semantic categories, those with *have* and *make* are less varied and especially linked to the category "speech." Moreover, observation of all nouns following *do*, *give*, *have*, *make*, and *take* suggests that some deverbal nouns can be used with more than one light verb, as is the case of *take care* and *have care*, inspiring questions concerning the extent to which these combinations are historically related to each other and characterized by linguistic competition. These topics will be examined in the next paragraph.

3.3.2 *The use of deverbal nouns with more than one verb*

The semantic characterization of light verbs and their dependency on the nominal component favor the use of various bases with identical nouns with no or limited semantic differences. This is the case of *have care/take care*, *have account/take account/give account*, *give answer/have answer/make answer*, and *have use/make use*, which often stand in paradigmatic competition sharing similar contextual features. Some examples are included in (12)–(18):

(12) and for that reason I **have the care of** them till the account is past. (1750s)
(13) I told them when I went out **to take care of** the doors. (1770s)
(14) The lady could **give no answer**. (1810s)

(15) I **had no answer** from him. (1770s)
(16) he **made no answer**. (1830s)

(17) he always **had the use of** my chest to put in his linen and his clothes. (1790s)
(18) and laying them on the table, said he **had no further use** for them (1810s)
(19) He **made use of** many oaths, and said he would blow our brains out (1750s)

Examination of examples (12)–(13) reveals that *have care* and *take care* both convey the meaning of "look after" and are often followed by the preposition *of*. Beyond these similarities, however, there are some divergences concerning the use of the article, which is especially prerogative of *have care*. Similarly, the CPs *give answer*, *have answer*, and *make answer* are characterized by the same pattern but they preserve some divergences when examined semantically. This is an important aspect because it weakens the principle, one form one meaning, supported within the structuralistic approaches (Anttila 1989) and enhances the unpredictability of words' senses that are construed in the linguistic context (Sinclair 1991). The use of *give answer* and *make answer* are, in this view, identical in form but it seems that they differ semantically since the former implies an action made passively in response to an external request whereas the latter entails the absence of that; At the same time, *have answer* is characterized by another connotation related to epistemic possibility rather than factual actions.

Considerations provided for *make answer/have answer/give answer* also apply to *have use/make use* because they do share similarities in use but they still preserve some peculiarities and diverse linguistic behaviors: *make use* seems to be lexicalized as a single fixed unit whereas *have use* is characterized by variable uses: the nominal component may be preceded by the article *the*, as in (17) above, or occur without it, as in (18), showing diverse degrees of internal cohesion. Diachronically, this means that the combinations exhibit diverse degrees of lexicalization, which corroborates the link between LModE and early times. Indeed, since ME CPs showed diverse degrees of fixity and, thus, lexicalization as proven by Sánchez Roura (2003: 197) highlighting that "from the distribution and frequency of noun modification, some collocations are found to be still free, in that they combine with a variety of modifiers, whereas others are already more fixed and are used with either the zero article or the indefinite article." There could be, in this respect, ongoing processes of innovation in LModE that favor linguistic competition between alternative forms characterized by diverse degrees of fixity and that may promote over time the establishment of one of the two forms or even the development of functional differences between them.

The possibility of using alternative forms is not a typical phenomenon of the LModE time, since it is also attested in the previous years when the various bases established a linguistic competition. As Akimoto and Brinton note (1999), the nominal components of the CPs of OE they examine can occur with more than one base verb, and some nouns even combine with three diverse bases, like *weg*, which is preceded by *don*, *niman*, and *habban*, or *sige*, which occurs with *sellan*, *niman*, and *habban*. Similar considerations apply to the other periods, such as ME when *part* combines with *do* and *have*, and *will* follows *do*, *have*, and *make* (Tanabe 1999), or the more recent EModE characterized by the interchangeability of verbal forms (Kytö 1999). Specifically, during the years 1500–1710 examined by Kytö (1999: 192, 193) there are many examples of "multiple use of nouns," including *have care* and *take care*, that are considered as verbs characterized by "differences in the semantic shades" and semantic specialization favoring the use of the former with the meaning of "be careful" and the latter with that of " attending to the issues referred to."

The substitution of some CPs formed with a common nominal component that is found in the *LModE-OBC* corroborates the link between these verbs and other multi-word verbs, which are featured with processes of layering over the years, especially phrasal verbs. In this regard, Leone (2023) investigates the use of the phrasal verbs formed with *forth*, *on*, and *out* over the EModE period and proves that there were processes of interferences and phenomena of semantic specialization driving the phrasal verbs formed with *forth*. In this instance, it is highlighted that the semantic similarities between alternative forms, together with ongoing processes of conventionalization of new shades of meanings, characterizing phrasal verbs with *on* and *out*, worked as catalysts for the disappearance of *forth*. Specifically, the catalyst of change was, in this case, the process of retraction intended as "in some sense the opposite of expansion in grammaticalization" (Haspelmath 2004: 33) and "the process that favors the obsolescence of instances or specific uses after a period of expansion" (Leone 2022: 2). These considerations may find application in the cases under discussion here since the pairs differ in terms of frequency, as shown in Table 3.3.

Table 3.3 Have care/take care and *have use/make use*: Raw frequency over the decades

	have care	take care	have use	make use
1750s	2	46	2	12
1770s	2	29	–	16
1790s	5	24	–	6
1810s	8	13	2	2
1830s	3	20	–	6
Total	20	132	4	42

Observation of the distribution of the pairs over the decades gives proof of a discrepancy between the selected CPs and reveals that *take care* and *make use* are far more frequent in the data than *have care* and *have use*. A possible explanation of the diverse rate could be the consequence of increasing use of *take care* and *make use* at the expense of *have care* and *have use* and their conventionalization over time. This is a hypothesis confirmed by the fact that *take care* and *make use* are more frequent than *have care* and *have use* in the years 1500–1710 as noted by Kytö (1999). The EModE time was, in this respect, characterized by a decline of *have care* and *have use* and by increasing use of CPs at the expense of their simple verb alternatives, such as *to use* and *to care* (Kytö 1999). The identification of the factors determining the retraction of some CPs is rather complex but it is possible at least to make some hypotheses. For example, Wang (2019) notes that *have care* can occur with *a*, *the*, or other determiners, whereas *take care* shows a more limited variability, since it combines with *the* or occurs without any determiner; This could entail that the degree of variability and fixedness may favor or, conversely, limit the use of a CP and determine processes of retraction. In this regard, it is also possible to hypothesize that a linguistic cycle occurs when "a regular pattern of language, a round of linguistic changes" operates "in a systematic manner and direction" (van Gelderen 2013: 233), and motivates change on CPs linked by a relation of synonymy.

These considerations are invaluable when examining cases of linguistic competition but they also work as the spot where variation meets changes, enhancing the principle whereby the more variation, the more the change. Indeed, the limited variability of *take care* may be a sign of a stronger degree of lexicalization because one of the prominent features of lexicalized forms is that they do not allow significant variation (Sánchez Roura 2003; Brinton & Traugott 2005; Wang 2019). At the same time, processes of retraction may be motivated by linguistic productivity as also noted by Leone (2022) about phrasal verbs formed with *forth* and discussed above. If this is the case, then *have*, *make*, and *take* could exhibit diverse productivity which is closely linked to the ability of a base to combine with nominal parts. This introduces the need to examine all CPs in terms of TTR which is the topic of the next paragraph.

3.3.3 Productivity

The quantitative description of the evolution of CPs over the years needs to be complemented with considerations of the degree of

38 Linguistic features

productivity exhibited by the single groups. Both Rf and Nf may give information on the tendencies followed by CPs but they also need to be interpreted in association with the ability of a base verb to occur with nouns to create CPs, which can be expressed using the TTR. Specifically, TTR "expresses the proportion of types (different word forms) relative to the proportion of tokens (running words)" and can reveal the degree of productivity of an item: "a larger number of different word forms (types) relative to the number of all words in text (tokens) points to a lexically more varied text" (Brezina 2018: 57). Overall, this means that calculating the lexical variation of a base verb is a crucial step to the understanding of changes affecting linguistic items over time, and to evaluate cases of retraction as those hypothesized in Section 3.3.2. It can be supposed that the greater the lexical variation, the more the productivity of the item and its ability to combine with other instances to promote innovation.

Moreover, measuring the degree of productivity of the base verbs could also give further information on the path followed by instances. On the one hand, there could be base verbs being very frequent, which may be characterized by limited productivity, meaning that the rates are due to the repetition of a single type. On the other hand, a decrease in frequency could be interpreted as related to ongoing changes but only when the TTR is marked.

Based on these considerations, I have calculated the TTR of each light verb in the *LModE-OBC*, which is represented in Table 3.4.

The analysis of the TTR of CPs over the years 1750–1850 reveals that *do* and *make* are the verbs characterized by the highest degree of productivity, reaching 0.19 and 0.13 respectively, which are followed by *have* with TTR 0.11. The other two verbs, *give* and *take*, only reach the rate of 0.09 and 0.04 respectively, which is indicative of very limited productivity.

The results obtained show that during the LModE period, there is variation among the various bases, which suggests the possibility of ongoing innovation further corroborating the conceptualization of this period as a time characterized by both stability and change (Hundt

Table 3.4 Type/Token Ratio of base verbs

do	give	have	make	take
0.19	0.09	0.11	0.13	0.04

2014; Leone 2023). Moreover, this hypothesis is enhanced by comparative analysis of rates exhibited by the bases *do*, *give*, *have*, *make*, and *take* during the years 1750–1850, with those of EModE reported by Kytö (1999) in her study on CPs occurring in the *Helsinki Corpus of English Texts*. Specifically, Kytö (1999) highlights that *do* and *take* are the bases with the most limited degree of productivity, at 0.24 and 0.26 respectively; At the same time, *give* has TTR 0.34, whereas *make* and *have* reach 0.36. Combining these rates with those examined so far reveals that all the verbs in LModE have variable TTRs: *take* is the least productive basis, whereas *make* is similar to but it does not have the same rate of *have*, while *give* exhibits a very low rate. An important factor is that in LModE the base verb *do* is characterized by the highest rate, whereas it occupies the third position in the ranking examined by Kytö (1999). The discrepancies attested when examining the TTR in comparative terms prove that CPs are still affected by innovation in the years 1750–1850 and that all bases have a more limited degree of productivity in LModE, granting it the status of a time showing increasing stabilization.

When considering the TTRs of the bases *have*, *make*, and *take*, which are part of the alternative CPs examined in Section 4.2.3, that is, *have care/take care*, and *make use/have use*, it is possible to exclude that the degree of productivity has played a role in the retraction of *have care* and *have use*. There could have been other factors favoring processes of retraction that may include the lexico-semantic features as is already the case of the phrasal verbs formed with *forth/on/out* examined by Leone (2022).

To avoid the potential influence of one single decade on the overall productivity of each group, I have calculated the TTR for each decade, as reported in Table 3.5.

Table 3.5 Type/Token Ratio of base verbs per decade

	do	give	have	make	take
1750s	0.25	0.22	0.31	0.31	0.11
1770s	0.47	0.17	0.31	0.26	0.12
1790s	0.53	0.20	0.27	0.40	0.11
1810s	0.36	0.22	0.32	0.45	0.17
1830s	0.29	0.21	0.21	0.30	0.16

40 Linguistic features

The TTR calculated per decade allows us to exclude the hypothesis whereby one single decade has determined the overall results. This implies, overall, that there are signs of stability in the behavior of each of the bases but also ongoing innovation.

4 Composite predicates between stability and change

4.1 Stable composite predicates

Many CPs found in the *LModE-OBC* exhibit stable features, which is evident from the comparison between instances dating back to the years 1750–1850 and those of PDE. For example, this is the case of verbs like *take hold of*, *take a walk*, *do justice*, *do action*, *make*, *excuse*, *make enquiry*, *have access*, *have evidence*, *have opinion*, *give account*, *give answer*, but the list would become larger if the intention is to mention all stable verbs. For practical reasons, to prove this aspect I have taken three verbs as case studies, that is, *take care*, *take notice*, and *take account*, as in (1)–(3). I also queried the untagged version of the *ARCHER* corpus, and, specifically, I have selected the section including British English dating back to 1950–1999, as in (4)-(6):

(1) I **take care of** my children. (1770s)
(2) I **took no account of** the numbers myself (1830s)
(3) I **took** particular **notice of** the house. (1770s)
(4) I was just into Dublin to help **take care of** her little brothers and sisters. (*ARCHER* 1968donl_f8b)
(5) The statutory hypothesis does not require, or make room for, the court also **to take account of** the appointment in favour of Timothy (*ARCHER* 1989inla_l8b)
(6) I didn't **take** much **notice of** it at the time (*ARCHER* 1961 simp_d8b)

Examination of the instances reported in (1)–(6) reveals that *take care*, *take notice* and *take account* have identical syntactic form and meaning, which further corroborates the status of the LModE time as

DOI: 10.4324/9781003410256-4

a stable period. Indeed, LModE has often been associated with limited innovation up to more recent years. However, since the 2010s a new debate around the proximity between LModE and PDE has stimulated increasing interest within the scientific community, resulting in several studies proving that the LModE time was far from being fixed (Nevalainen 2006 Hundt 2014). As suggested in the preceding chapters, however, observation of stable uses does not exclude the existence of ongoing innovation, as will be proved in the following sections.

4.2 Morpho-syntactic features of composite predicate

4.2.1 Syntactic patterns

During the years 1750–1850 CPs followed two patterns, that is, verb + noun and verb + noun + preposition, which is a sign of continuity between early times and PDE. Indeed, the occurrence of these two patterns is attested since ME (Matsumoto 1999) and remained stable over time.

Verb + Noun pattern. Verbs following this pattern can occur either in the form verb + noun or verb + determiner + noun, that is, CPs may function as a fixed combination or permit internal lexical variation. Some examples of verbs belonging to this group are *have fit, have hurt, have deal, take a walk, take place, make mistake, make attempt, give information, give judgment, do a robbery, do a deal*, as in (7)–(9):

(7) I understood you to say, that this conversation **took place** in the public-house? (1790s)
(8) Yea I did not **give any information** about that to any policeman that struck me when I went on board (1830s)
(9) It is very odd he should say so – he must **have made a mistake** (1810s)

Verb + Noun + Preposition pattern. CPs included in this group are, for example, *have opinion of, have warrant from/against, have suspicion of, take account of, take advantage of, make observation of, make mention of, give answer to, do job for*, as in (10)–(12):

(10) The prisoner never **made mention of** a man being with us, neither there or at the justice's; it is all false. (1750s)

(11) Is it your custom **to take account of** the articles delivered to the men? (1810s)
(12) so he **took the advantage of** me to get money out of me. (1750s)

Moreover, similar to PDE, there are CPs that allow alternative patterns, like *give notice*, which can occur as verb + noun pattern, as in (13), or as verb + noun + preposition pattern, as in (14)–(15), where it can occur with the preposition *of* or *to* depending on the features of the following noun: *to* precedes nouns referring to humans, whereas *of* is used to introduce activities or objects.

(13) He absconded the 7th of December, and **gave no notice** when he went away (1750s)
(14) **Had he given** you **any notice of** going away (1810s)
(15) my drawers were not kept locked I **gave notice to** the police (1830s)

Similar considerations apply to the CP *have mercy* which, in addition to being used in the pattern verb + noun, , also occurs with the prepositions *on/upon* and *for*, as in (16)–(18):

(16) she said, Lord **have mercy upon** me! poor creatures (1750s)
(17) I hope you will **have mercy on** me. (1830s)
(18) I leave myself to the mercy of the Court, seeing my friends **have no mercy for** me. (1810s)

These are a few examples of CPs allowing variation and diverse syntactic structures but the number increases when extending the analysis to all bases considered in the present study: *take care, take notice, take effect of/on/upon, make observation on/upon/of, make an assault, give appearance to/of, give liberty, give answer*.
Similarly to PDE, in LModE *take care* was used as either verb + noun or verb + noun + preposition, as in (19)–(20):

(19) I **took care** they never should get together. (1770s)
(20) I have three small children; I **take care of** my children. (1770s)

The existence of various syntactic realizations seems to be a well-attested feature of CPs of the years 1750–1850, which further corroborates the link between LModE and PDE without, however, demystifying the importance of ongoing innovation and operativeness of processes of lexicalization, as I will demonstrate in Chapter 5.

4.2.2 Articles and determiners

As suggested in Chapter 1, the occurrence of a determiner, especially articles, allows the grouping of CPs into two patterns: (i) CPs are occurring as verb + noun; (ii) CPs are occurring as verb + noun, which may be preceded and followed by other components, that is, definite and indefinite articles *a/an/the*, possessive pronouns like *her/his/their*, determiners like *this/that*, or *many/such*, and *no*.

The occurrence of CPs with the article is considered to be a prototypical feature of CPs in PDE (Stein & Quirk 1991) whereas article-less CPs are seen as "a subpattern of this category" (Wang 2019: 40). Indeed, these two categories are closely linked to each other from a diachronic perspective and it is possible to hypothesize that the alternative use of an article or article-less CP may be indicative of ongoing change and, specifically, of lexicalization of combinations: if "one way to examine the extent a CP is syntactically fossilized is by checking the occurrence of modifiers and determiners" (Wang 2019: 40), then the occurrence of alternative patterns may be the *locus* of change. The lexical component of some CPs was stabilized by EModE, whereas there was still variation concerning the use of articles and determiners up to the seventeenth century (Matsumoto 2005; Wang 2019). This means that, hypothetically, there are rather stable features in LModE that combine with limited changes.

To examine the use of determiners and evaluate the extent to which the LModE time is affected by change, CPs have been divided into four groups: (i) CPs with articles *a/an/the* (V+Art+N); (ii) CPs without articles (V+Ø+N); (iii) CPs with other determiners like *some/any/many/other* and *this/that/these/those* (V+D+N); (iv) CPs with personal pronouns (V+Pp+N). Then the rates of CPs have been calculated in each case and compared with those reported in a study on CPs of the EModE period. Specifically, the reference is here to the study undertaken by Wang (2009) on CPs during the years 1560–1760, who queries the data in the *CED* (Kytö & Walker 2006), including speech recordings of trials, rendering the results comparable with

Table 4.1 Articles and determiners of composite predicates (%)

	V+ArtN	V+Ø+N	V+D+N	V+Pp+N
do	32.72	20	9.09	38.18
give	50.33	34.67	3.34	11.64
have	35.78	44.34	0.87	18.99
make	42.12	33.64	7.67	16.55
take	20.07	74.29	1.87	3.75
Total	38.04	43.72	3.61	14.61

those included in the present study. Table 4.1 includes CPs grouped according to their morpho-syntactic patterns.

Similarly to EModE (Wang 2019), the most common pattern is the use of CPs without any article, which is immediately followed by CPs including an article. This is a well-attested tendency that also characterizes ME and early times when the zero article is the most common determiner, "although a decrease in its use can be detected chronologically" (Moralejo Gàrate 2002: 176; Wang 2019). However, since then, this pattern has steadily declined in use, which explains why "the prototypical pattern for CPs in Present Day English has been repeatedly claimed to consist of a verb followed by an indefinite noun phrase" (Moralejo Gàrate 2002: 176). The fact that the years immediately preceding PDE are characterized by the prominence of CPs without an article/determiner acquires particular value because it enhances the status of LModE as a period as linguistically unstable and close to earlier periods. It is interesting to note that there is variation among the various bases and that the overall count of V+Art+N and V+Ø+N patterns contrasts the tendency attested in PDE. That is to say that, despite some bases overall exhibiting the same tendency of CPs in PDE with the prominence of the second pattern like *have* and *take*, the others do not, which enhances the existence of ongoing changes in the years 1750–1850. This hypothesis is corroborated by the fact that *have* and *take* are characterized by increasing use in their V+Ø+N pattern in the period that immediately precedes LModE, that is EModE. In this regard, Wang (2019) reports that the use of the pattern V+Ø+N with these two bases shows increasing rates over the years 1560–1760, which places the results obtained in the *LModE-OBC* in direct relation with the previous rather than following times. The prominence for the V+Ø+N pattern is also common to CPs attested back to ME when 50.53% of verbs occur with this pattern as reported by Moralejo Gàrate (2002: 175) in his study on CPs undertaken on the ME prose and verse included in the *Helsinki Corpus of English Texts*. All of this has two consequences: (i) in LModE the bases show diverse behavior which entails that they each preserve their linguistic identity and syntactic preference; (ii) CPs of LModE are at an intermediate stage in their syntactic fixing, that is they are placed between earlier times when the zero article pattern dominates and PDE when the opposite tendency is attested.

As for the use of other determiners, the LModE time is similar to other periods in the history of English. Specifically, the use of CPs with more than one of the mentioned determiners is not an isolated phenomenon, neither in LModE nor in EModE (Wang 2019): many combinations occur alternatively with one or the other one or even the combination of them. For example, *give answer* may occur with an article, as in (21), or an article followed by an adjective, as in (22); Alternatively, it can be used in combination with various determiners, as in (23), where it also allows the insertion of the pronoun *her* and be part of a ditransitive pattern.

(21) We answered we would call, and **give an answer** in the morning (1810s)
(22) he did **not give a decided answer** (1830s)
(23) he **gave her some surly answer**. (1770s)

Give answer is only one of the many CPs allowing diverse uses which may occur with one or more modifiers, such as *have deal, have knowledge, take care, take notice, make excuse, make haste, give account, do work*, and *do job*, to name a few. In this respect, the linguistic behavior of CPs is not dissimilar from that of modern times, which is a feature that CPs acquired back to ME (Matsumoto 1999; Tanabe 1999). This creates, once again, a line of continuity in the use of CPs over time, which unlocks the importance of studying both stability and change in language use. Often there are structures and uses that were established in early times which remain stable and may favor processes of change or give rise to the establishment of new uses as it is the case of CPs used as part of fixed more complex combinations allowing internal modification, as I will describe in the next section.

Composite predicates between stability and change 47

4.2.3 *Internal modification*

CPs of the LModE period discussed in Section 4.1. demonstrate that, similar to other multi-word verbs of the time (Leone 2023), many CPs had acquired stability in early times. The existence of stable features also concerns the nominal component and the possibility of intervening objects, like adjectives. Internal modification is, indeed, a linguistic characteristic associated with CPs (Jespersen 1942) since early times as proved by scholars like Matsumoto (1999), Hiltunen (1999), and Kytö (1999).

In terms of frequency, modification of CPs included in the *LModE-OBC* is not a very common phenomenon and especially characterizes CPs which include the determiner *a/an/the*. The rates of CPs occurring with an intervening element are attested to not more than 22.81% in all bases, as reported in Table 4.2.

The bases forming CPs that exhibit the most prominent tendency to occur with adjectives and modifiers are *do* and *give*, followed by *have* and then *take* and *make*. However, the examination of the types allowing modification reveals that there are some CPs that influence the overall result, making the rates, in some respects, biased. For example, *take* is characterized by many occurrences of *take notice* (Rf 65 out of 123 hits) allowing modification. At the same time, *give account* (35 out of 105 hits) and *give character* (96 out of 143 hits) influence the percentage reported for *give*. This overall means that specific CPs are showing a "propensity" to occur with intervening elements, which are also identical in almost all cases. Specifically, *good* and *great* are the most common adjectives occurring in CPs, even though there are others like *excellent*, *same*, *secure*, *ordinary*, *particular*, *least*, and *different*, which variously collocate with the following nouns. Some examples of CPs with modifiers are reported in (24)–(26):

Table 4.2 Modification of composite predicates (%)

do	give	have	make	take
22.81	21.68	13.39	10.49	12.94

48   *Composite predicates between stability and change*

(24) that if I **made the least resistance** he would call a third man (1770s)
(25) he wanted the young man to **do a private job** for him (1750s)
(26) It **made a tinkling noise** about ten minutes after that the prisoner came out of the cellar (1830s)

The considerations provided have two major implications: (i) CPs of the LModE time exhibit a behavior that is similar to that attested since ME; (ii) some CPs are part of fixed expressions rendering them phraseologically complex combinations.

First, the fact that CPs occur with *great* and *good* acquires relevance when the results are contextualized within the literature since there are studies that have demonstrated that the use of modifying adjectives, and, in particular, the use of these mentioned adjectives is one of the "abiding characteristics of CPs" (Matsumoto 1999: 83). Specifically, the reference here is to the results obtained by Matsumoto (1999) in her studies on CPs of ME and ModE who states that *gret(e, good* is used very frequently in combination with CPs, and that they play "the role of emphasizer" (Matsumoto 1999: 83; Tanabe 1999). Indeed, the adjective does not modify the meaning of the verb + noun combination which forms a phraseological unit but it functions as an operator that intensifies the meaning already portrayed by the CP: for example, *take reward* differs from *take good reward* because the adjective moves the meaning from "to take into account" to that of "to take full account of," as highlighted by Matsumoto (1999). Similar considerations apply to the cases found in the *LModE-OBC*, as in (27)–(28), where *make noise* occurs with or without *great* functioning as an emphasizer:

(27) and kept whiffing the smoke about and **making a noise** with his feet (1810s)
(28) and he shook it, and **made a great noise,** which could be heard by any person on the landing (1830s)

In examples (27)–(28), the adjective *great* intensifies what is already expressed by the CP and determines a slight semantic shift. At the same time, the additional use of an adjective like *great* also affects the internal cohesion of the CP. As Matsumoto highlights (1999: 83), the adjective weakens the cohesion in a very limited way, differently from other adjectives like *true*, or content modifiers like *excellent*, *different*, and *ordinary*, which affect the cohesion in a more significant way. The semantic characteristics of the adjectives seem to determine the meaning of the whole combination: while adjectives like *good* and *great* portray a very general meaning, the other already mentioned adjectives convey more specific meanings, which means that they semantically play a major role within the combinations working as factors that weaken the cohesion.

Adopting a diachronic approach, the possibility of modification may signal the evolution of a combination because, as suggested, the occurrence of modifiers may affect the cohesion and thus may reveal the degree of lexicalization of a combination. Moreover, there are also cases where the adjective occurs in its comparative and superlative form *more/the most*, or with *such* falling in the category of "numerous, big" as defined by Tanabe (1999: 115). Also in this case, the cohesion between the verb and the following noun seems to be weakened, which introduces the second aspect mentioned above concerning the establishment of some CPs allowing modification as fixed phraseological forms.

The examination of CPs occurring with a modifier in the *LModE-OBC* reveals that some CPs show a preference to occur with one or more adjectives, forming fixed expressions. This is the case of *have a good mind, have a great deal, give a good character, take particular/great notice, make a great noise, make the best of my way*, as in (29)–(31):

(29) it **made a great noise** and ratling in the dining room (1770s)
(30) The prisoner **had a great deal of** faith to trust you 6 l. 10 s. (1750s)

For example, 5 out of 7 instances of *make* allowing adjectival modification occur with the adjective *great*, as in (29), whereas 13 out of 13 instances of *make* followed by the noun *way* is used as a fixed expression *make the best of my way*. Similarly, 10 out of 11 instances of *has* combined with *deal* is used as *have a great deal*, as in (30). The use of CPs with specific and recurrent adjectival modification acquires particular value because it should be hypothesized that *great* and *good*, in addition to being the most versatile adjectives in CPs in terms of frequency since ME (Matsumoto 1999), also form phraseological phrases. These assertions entail that within the approach to phraseology of the Sovietic school (Cowie 1998) CPs are phraseological forms, that is, they are composed of a verb and a noun (plus determiners) functioning as lexemes, which tend to combine with particular adjectives and to occur as fixed expressions, as those already discussed.

4.2.4 The use of plural forms

Similarly to EModE (Kytö 1999; Wang 2019), CPs occurring in the *LModE-OBC* are especially characterized by singular nouns, which once again proves that the years 1750–1850 are very close to previous times. Despite the similarity in the trend, however, data included in the *LModE-OBC* show signs of ongoing innovation: the rates of CPs occurring with a plural noun are very limited, and they are much less frequent than those recorded in Kytö's (1999) study on EModE. Specifically, she states that almost all the CPs of EModE are composed of singular nouns, which represent more than 88% of all instances for each basis *make, take, do, have, give*. Differently, the rates in the LModE are no less than 93.57%, which means that there is a drop in the use of plural nouns. The rates of CPs occurring with singular nouns are reported in Table 4.3 along with the rates calculated by Kytö (1999) in her work on CPs of the EModE period.

A comparison of the rates of CPs occurring with singular nouns in the two temporal periods reveals that the percentages are high in both cases but there is an increasing trend in LModE. This is a very interesting aspect because the limited number of plural forms may reveal a tendency towards grammaticalization and lexicalization (Wang 2019). Acceptance of these considerations should be speculative, however, without further research. These processes and cases of lexicalization/grammaticalization will be examined in Chapter 5.

Table 4.3 Percentages of singular nouns in EModE and LModE

	EModE	LModE
do	88	93.63
give	91	95.55
have	86	97.25
make	91	94.88
take	90	99.24

Composite predicates between stability and change 51

For ease of reference, following the approach taken by Kytö (1999), I will report some examples of CPs that only occur with singular nouns, or are used alternatively with one or the other form.

a. Verb + singular noun
Do: *service, justice, favour, damage*
Give: *information, reference, possession*
Have: *discourse, idea, intention, pleasure*
Make: *attempt, stroke, remark, difference*
Take: *hold, notice, possession, place, care*

b. Verb + plural or singular noun
Do: *robbery, job, action*
Give: *order, notice, reason, word, verdict*
Have: *charge, dealing, question, impression*
Make: *excuse, promise, information*
Take: *account, charge*

The possibility of exclusive or alternative uses has been a typical feature of CPs since early times (Kytö 1999). Indeed, *make friends* and *make amends*, which are always used with plural nouns in EModE, also occur in their plural forms in LModE, as in (31)–(32).

(31) the captain will **make you amends**. (1750s)
(32) By being down at that house I **have made all my friends** my foes. (1790s)

A point of divergence is that these verbs both occur as *hapax legomena* in LModE. Another difference lies in the absence of *make answers, take courses, do favours/miracles/offices/works* which are, instead, reported in Kytö's (1999: 181) work. This scholar also mentions *give direction(s)* stating that 3 out of 7 hits occur in the plural form, which is similar to what happens in LModE, when 12 out 28 instances occur with the nominal part set in its plural form.

4.2.5 Passivization

The verb + noun (+ preposition) of CPs form an indivisible unit that ideally admits passive, as in (33)–(34):

(33) Direction was given to prove the state of mind he was in at the time **the attempt was made** upon Mr. Miller. (1770s)
(34) **The reply that was made** from within, I cannot tell. (1790s)

The use of passive in CPs is, however, a very rare phenomenon since CPs are almost exclusively used in their active pattern, as shown in Table 4.4. I calculated the raw frequency and percentages of passive forms per decade by excluding the *there*-passive constructions: the reason lies in the fact that the aim was to focus on passivization as a sign of the degree of lexicalization of instances. The inclusion of *there*-passive combinations, in this respect, would have not allowed evaluation of the topicalization of nouns and of the strength of internal cohesion.

The rates reported in Table 4.4 corroborate the stability characterizing CPs over time and create a line of continuity between the very recent LModE period and OE when CPs were almost exclusively used in their active form (Matsumoto 1999; Tanabe 1999; Brinton 2008). The fact that passivization is not allowed in most of the cases and that, when it occurs, inner passive is the only type of transformation allowed, enhances the phraseological status of CPs and the internal cohesion of components (Brinton 2008: 24). Overall, the linguistic behavior registered since OE, in this respect, proves that these combinations that were first established in many cases as a calque from Latin (Akimoto & Brinton 1999; see also Iglesias-Ránabe 2001), endorsed processes of lexicalization strengthening the internal cohesion and partly impeding passivization.

In terms of frequency, each basis is characterized by limited use of passive over the decades, which are dominated by *do* (10%) followed

Table 4.4 Passive form (%) and raw frequency (n)

	do	give	have	make	take
1750s	2 (2)	0.13 (1)	–	0.53 (4)	0.56 (3)
1770s	0.90 (1)	0.66 (5)	–	1.74 (13)	0.37 (2)
1790s	2.72 (3)	–	–	1.47 (11)	–
1810s	3.63 (4)	0.40 (3)	–	0.94 (7)	0.18 (1)
1830s	0.90 (1)	1.20 (9)	-	2.01 (15)	-
Total	10 (11)	2.40 (18)	-	6.72 (50)	1.12 (6)

Composite predicates between stability and change   53

by *make*, *give*, and *take*, whereas there are no occurrences of *have* in its passive form. This is an interesting aspect that works as a dividing line between the LModE period and the previous periods. The basis *have* is never used in its passive form in the years 1750–1850 whereas it occurs in 4 matches in the *Paston Letters* as noted by Tanabe (1999) in ME. At the same time, *make* and *take* are the most frequent bases used in the passive form in ME whereas *take* shows limited rates in LModE. The linguistic behavior remained stable during the EModE period when only the inner passive is attested (Claridge 2000). There are no other elements that emerge from the examination of the data included in the *LModE-OBC* to prove that there is a link between lexicalization and passive; However, it is possible to make some generalizations and hypothesize that CPs and their uses fluctuate over the years with a trend featured with expansion and retraction in a linguistic cycle that always characterizes language change (van Gelderen 2013).

4.3 Semantic features

CPs occurring in the *LModE-OBC* exhibit features that are already attested in EModE and described by Kytö (1999) and Claridge (2000), and share properties that also characterize other multi-word verbs, including phrasal verbs, prepositional verbs, and phrasal-prepositional verbs of the time (Leone 2023). Indeed, when contextualizing CPs within the multi-word verb system, it is possible to note that they show meanings ranging on a cline of idiomaticity, that is, instances are showing idiomatic meanings, other semi-compositional meanings whereas at the extreme pole, there are CPs with literal connotation. The reference here is to the studies undertaken by Claridge (2000) and Kytö (1999) stating that, for example, verbs like *have account* belong to the first group, as in (35), whereas verbs like *take place* and *make haste* are categorized as members of the second and third mentioned groups respectively, as in (36)–(37):

(35) If you **have any account** to give of yourself to the jury, where you was. (1790s)
(36) I understood you to say, that this conversation **took place** in the public-house? (1790s)
(37) he wished me to **make haste**. (1810s)

According to the *OED*, *take place* means "to take effect, succeed" (*OED*, v. *take place*), whereas *make haste* means "to move or act quickly" (*OED*, v. *make haste*) with *haste* conveying the meaning of "excessive speed of motion or action" (*OED*, v. *haste*). Moreover, in both cases, the noun is metaphorically linked to the preceding basis rendering its meaning partly non-compositional. At the same time, there is no proper entry for *have account*, which is indicative of its more limited lexicalized status and its compositional connotation.

The existence of CPs exhibiting different degrees of compositionality is the point of departure for the evaluation of changes affecting the semantics of these verbs over the years 1750–1850. Indeed, CPs have often been seen as placed "somewhere in the middle of the magnetic field of language [...] where grammar and lexis meet" (Algeo 1995: 203), and affected variously by grammaticalization and lexicalization (Brinton 2008) and changes in the degree of compositionality (Traugott 1999). These aspects stress the importance of treating CPs as diachronically linked to all the mentioned processes of change, which is the topic of the next Chapter.

5 Processes of change

5.1 Grammaticalization and lexicalization

The conceptualization of CPs as placed in the middle between grammar and lexis is the point of departure to examine CPs and contribute to the existing debates concerning whether and the extent to which these verbs are the result of grammaticalization (Brinton 2008), lexicalization (Traugott 1999) or a mixture of the two (Trousdale 2008). CPs should be examined as the result of a complex process theorized by Akimoto (1989) and revisited by Traugott (1999), validating the existence of four steps: (1) CPs occur as phrasal constructions with compositional meaning; (2) CPs function as examples of phrasal lexicalization with stable co-occurrence of the base verb and the nominal part; (3) CPs are combinations undergoing syntactic and semantic reanalysis; (4) CPs establish as idiomatic combinations with syntactic fixity. Acceptance of the operativeness of this complex process has several consequences: (i) grammaticalization and lexicalization of the components are closely linked to each other; (ii) lexicalization endorses also idiomatization, as CPs that lexicalized inevitably acquire new meanings and the combination undergoes semantic reanalysis and increasing non-compositionality; (iii) CPs may be placed anywhere along the cline of grammaticality/lexicality and may exhibit diverse degrees of idiomatization.

To examine these issues works undertaken so far, including those proposed by Wang (2019), have identified factors that are useful to describe the status of components and the internal cohesion, that is, the use of plural forms and the occurrence of modifiers and determines with the noun.

DOI: 10.4324/9781003410256-5

In the first case, the use of a plural nominal component may signal that the noun can vary morphologically and add inflectional morphemes to the root. The possibility of morphological variation weakens the internal cohesion between the constituents and affects the degree of fixity of the V+N combination that is one of the defining properties of phraseological forms: within lexical semantics, indeed, phraseological items should be units "characterised by internal stability and uninterruptability" (Lyons 1968: 202). This recalls the second aspect mentioned above concerning the use of determiners within the V+N combinations. The use of articles or determiners, along with the possibility of modification by adjectives and adverbs, once again may be signs of limited internal cohesion and reveal that the combination is not entirely lexicalized.

Reading these considerations in the light of the description given to CPs in this work seems to unlock contradictory views: CPs are lexemes but they allow the use of determiners and modifications and, thus, internal variation, which violates the idea of uninterruptability theorized by Lyons (1968) for lexemes. Objection to the criterion of fixedness comes from many scholars including Traugott (1999) and Brinton (2008) highlighting that a single CP may occur both with and without an article, and may also allow plural forms of the noun to preserve their lexeme status. An explanation for this contradictory definition of CPs lies in the fact that CPs are set in the middle between grammar and lexis and one of their main features is that they are grammaticalized and lexicalized at different degrees: thus, the use of articles, plural nouns, or modification does not affect the status of combinations working as a CP which are *sui generis* in this respect, but diachronically can help the identification of intermediate stages ended up in the establishment of CPs as they are used in PDE. The point of departure is that, if a combination shows a decreasing use with plural nouns, articles, and intervening objects, then that combination may be affected by increasing grammaticalization and lexicalization. This is why, in the absence of other criteria, the present study will adopt the consolidated perspective based on the occurrence of determiners and/or plural nouns to identify CPs affected by change and interpret the results critically in light of the limitations that this approach has.

Querying the *LModE-OBC* proves that grammaticalization and lexicalization affected some instances of CPs, which gradually increased their internal cohesion after the deletion of the determiner.

Specifically, they moved from use in the pattern V+D+N to that of V+Ø+N and, on many occasions, the second pattern became the preferred form. This is the case of verbs like *have evidence, have information, have use, have hearing, have acquaintance, have care, take notice, take account, take place, take charge, make evidence, make haste, make resistance, make information,* and *give information.*

Taking the verbs *have use, have information, take notice,* and *take place* as a case study, it is possible to observe the role performed by grammaticalization and lexicalization in the renewal of CPs and processes of deletion of the article.

As for *have use,* it is exclusively used as *have use* without a determiner, as in (1), except for the 1790s when one hit occurs with the article *the,* as in (2):

(1) she **had use** to come to my house for drink (1750s)
(2) he always **had the use of** my chest to put in his linen and his clothes. (1790s)

Similarly, *have information, take notice,* and *take place,* exhibit the preference for the pattern V+Ø+N, as in (3)–(5), whereas they also occur with the article *an/the,* as in (6)–(8):

(3) I **have had information** about another man, who has absconded. (1790s)
(4) Did not the prisoner say it was a lucky thing, when he produced the ring and receipt, and whether it **was not taken notice of** at that time? (1770s)
(5) I have told all that **took place** on this occasion (1830s)
(6) the day the property was lost, I **had an information of** the robbery (1790s)
(7) I never saw such a particular thing in a wig before, which made me **take the more notice of** it. (1770s)
(8) I took the harness home, then went, and **took the place** at the public-house (1830s)

The use of *take place* without an article is a typical feature of this CP in the *ARCHER* corpus, which is a pattern that is first attested in OE as specified by the *OED.* There are occurrences of *take the place,* however, which convey a different meaning: instead of conveying the meaning of "to happen" they are linked to the act of "substitution", as in (9). In the case of *take notice*, instead, there are no occurrences in the *ARCHER* where the CP only occurs as *take notice*, as in (10):

(9) And when the young ones gradually **take the place of** the old (*ARCHER* 1908yeat_d7b)
(10) But I advise you not **to take notice of** your knowing it (*ARCHER* 1701trot_d3b)

Ultimately, there are no occurrences of either *have information* or *have the/an information* in the *ARCHERi* which stimulates discussion concerning the reasons beyond the absence of both combinations. It is possible to hypothesize that the reason is ongoing innovation favoring decreasing use or even disappearance in the use of specific lexemes and/or patterns that is especially observable in speech-based genres included in the *LModE-OBC*.

These results confirm the close link between LModE and PDE: "even in PDE, articles in CPs sometimes drop out, as in *make a noise*, which has given rise to *make noise*, which itself seems to have become a kind of simple verb" (Matsumoto 2005: 450). The fact that some CPs occur with the patterns V+Ø+N but still preserve rare use with the article proves that there is increasing grammaticalization of the single components and lexicalization of the combination as a whole. Proof of the decategorialization of the nominal components lies, indeed, in the absence of articles, along with a limited number of adjectival modification, which are both signs of decategorialization (Trousdale 2008: 58).

If the results are contextualized within the four-stage process discussed above, it is possible to note that CPs are at the end pole of the process of both grammaticalization and lexicalization. Specifically, they are placed at the fourth stage characterized by the "reanalysis of the constituent structure" (Akimoto 1999: 16) moving from [V] [D] [N] to [V] [N], and the consequent lexicalization of the constituents into a single lexeme. Examining the constituents suggests that they qualify as grammaticalized structures that satisfy the criteria defined by Akimoto (1999: 17) and, in particular, that concerning "increasing bondedness with the verb, loss of syntactic variability, syntactic reanalysis of the construction." At the same time, these CPs are lexicalized as they endorse the path towards increasing lexicality, with lexicalization of a form defined as the univerbation of the components (Brinton & Traugott 2005).

The base verb and the noun started to occur as combinations showing an increasing internal cohesion, which is a defining property of lexicalization. The components, instead, grammaticalized and increased their bounded status. This is the point where grammar meets lexis and CPs become exemplar cases of the existence of gradience of lexicality and grammaticality in the language (Brinton & Traugott 2005): "the syntactic behaviour of composite predicates presents strong evidence for a gradience view of lexicality and grammaticality" (Brinton 2008: 50). Acceptance of these considerations entails that the present study partly takes distance from the discussion undertaken by Traugott (1999), and Brinton (2008), stating that CPs with *do*, *give*, *have*, *make*, and *take* are especially lexicalized and grammaticalized, respectively, and adopts that elaborated by Trousdale (2008), claiming that they are both grammaticalized and lexicalized.

Grammaticalization and lexicalization are, however, not the only processes working on CPs since, once formed, the combinations inevitably modify their semantic features and become more idiomatized. Overall this reveals the importance of grammaticalization, lexicalization and idiomatization in the renewal of CPs, and enhances their interdependency in language change. The linguistic features of CPs allowing diverse patterns, and the occurrence of CPs with or without a determiner which can be modified over time, corroborate the status of CPs as verbs placed in the middle of the continuum grammaticality/lexicality described by Brinton and Traugott (2005) where an affected item may move toward the lexical/contentful/non-productive pole or the grammatical pole.

5.2 Phraseological variation and layering between alternative prepositions

The degree of fixedness and lexicalization of CPs of the LModE time is measured by considering criteria like the use of plural nouns, the absence of the article, and internal modification, as already discussed, but also by examining phraseological variation involving the preposition. As described in Chapter 1, CPs are a group of verbs that may exhibit diverse internal structures because some verbs occur as V+N patterns which contrast those instances that, instead, are composed of V+N+preposition patterns. However, when examined diachronically, CPs are not easily categorized as members of one or the other group, and the reason lies in the fact that (i) CPs may move from the former to the latter group as a consequence of additional use of a preposition or lack of it; (ii) CPs may exhibit variation in the preposition without moving to the V+N group.

As for the first issue, the data included in the *LModE-OBC* do not give evidence of cases of shifting as CPs often have unpredictable behavior and can occur with both the V+N and V+N+preposition pattern, as is the case of *have reason* reported in (11)–(12):

(11) **Have** you any **reason** to believe that this gentleman had any malice against you so as to attempt a thing of this sort? (1770s)
(12) **Have** you any other **reason for** saying you believe Gunnell was there, than from his being dressed as a brewer's servant (1810s)

There are then CPs that, instead, may include diverse prepositions but the meaning of the combination remains unchanged. This is the case, for example, of CPs like *have concern in/with, have hold on/of/ upon, have advantage of/by, have use of/for, make inquiry of/about/ into, make observation on/upon/of/about, make entry of/in.* Some examples of *make observation* are reported in (13)–(16):

(13) Were you and Miller alone when he **made the observation about** splitting? (1830s)
(14) and **made some little observations upon** his behavior. (1770s)
(15) so that he could not **make any observation of** the persons. (1770s)
(16) which frightened me so much that I **made no observation on** his person. (1770s)

Examination of these instances reveals that the verb *make* is followed by the noun *observation* but the combination is not stable in terms of constituency as it can include many prepositions. The absence of meaning shifts is a key factor: the CP under investigation is still affected by ongoing innovation and has not reached fixedness during the years 1750–1850 and, thus, is not completely lexicalized. Further corroborating this hypothesis is the fact that *make observation on* and *make observation of* are attested up to the 1790s whereas *make observation about* is used in the 1830s, which suggests that the CP is involved in phenomena of layering ended up in the survival of one of the alternatives.

Similar considerations apply to other mentioned CPs, like *have concern*, as shown in (17)–(18):

(17) When I was before the Justice, this woman said I **had no concern with** her husband? (1770s)
(18) he **had no concern in** unloading the coach. (1790s)

Once again, the use of *have concern* followed by *with* and *in* seems not to affect the meaning of the CP, which proves the existence of layering between the forms. At the same time, the fact that the preposition *with* occurs only one hit in the 1770s corroborates the idea whereby the process of competition and detraction of the CP formed with this preposition was almost over during the years 1750–1850: there is a kind of linguistic cycle moving CPs towards increasing lexicalization, and fixedness also in the use of the preposition.

5.3 The coinage of new composite predicates

The examination of types over the decades reveals that there is a limited number of new CPs that were first established in the period 1750–1850 such as *have control, have belief, have hesitation, take warning, take trouble, take opinion, make statement, make discussion, make effort, make demand, do injustice, give possession, give reference*. Indeed, these verbs are not included in the list provided by Kytö (1999) in her study on EModE and do not occur in the *ARCHER* (both British and American Sections) at least up to 1750. This comes as proof of the fact that there are new coinages in LModE. The process that operates on CPs included in the *LModE-OBC* is analogy favoring the creation of new forms taking other already established CPs as models to follow (Hopper & Traugott 2003). Specifically, there are three major tendencies: (i) there are CPs which emerge in consequence of analogical processes favoring the use of a noun with other bases e.g. *take warning/have warning, take trouble/have trouble, take opinion/have opinion*; (ii) there are CPs which establish via analogy stimulating the use of a single basis with other nouns belonging to similar semantic field, e.g. *have control/have command, have belief/have idea, have hesitation/have doubt, make statement/make claim, make discussion/ make discourse, make demand/make request*; (iii) CPs are emerging as the result of analogical processes working between antonymous nominal parts, for example, *do justice/do injustice*. Despite the diversity of the models, all these verbs follow a similar path of development driven by analogy intended as either "the attraction of extant forms to already existing constructions" where new verbs establish via direct formation to fill the X in A:B=X:C, or analogical generalization occurring as "rule generalization" within the linguistic system (Hopper & Traugott 2003: 63–64, 65).

For example, members of the first of the mentioned groups include *take warning*, and *take opinion*, as in (19)–(20):

(19) he begged his companions to **take warning** by him, as they saw the situation he had brought himself into. (1770s)
(20) Yes when I wanted him I asked him to go, and **took** his **opinion** I gave him 260l. (1830s)

These verbs occur as *hapax legomena* in 1770 (*take warning*) and in 1830 (*take opinion*), which grants them the status of new coinages. This aspect is confirmed by the *ARCHER*, which first includes *take warning* in 1831, as in (21), and *take opinion* in 1776, as in (22). At the same time, there are no occurrences of these verbs in early studies like that of Kytö (1999), corroborating their innovative status.

(21) We must **take warning** (*ARCHER* 1831nem__n5a)
(22) as all parties were amicably before the Court to **take** its **opinion** (*ARCHER* 1776dick_l4b)

Observation of the meanings and uses of these CPs reveals that they are very close to other already established verbs like *have warning* and *have opinion*, which are attested in the 1750s, as in (22)–(23), and are also listed in EModE:

(22) I told her I **had a warning** (1750s)
(23) I always **had a great opinion** of his honesty. (1750s)

The similarity between forms and meanings of the new CPs and the other well-attested CPs enhances the analogical link between these instances since linguistic similarity is a defining feature of analogical processes (Anttila 1989). Direct formation is, in this case, the complementary mechanism that favored the use of the nouns *warning* and *opinion* with other bases via proportional analogy and promoted the establishment of new members of CPs. Thus, the use of CPs with similar linguistic features, along with the fact that the alternatives are conventionalized forms, functions as proof of analogical processes that worked on the English verb system of the time.

Similar considerations apply to CPs included in the second and third groups, and the only difference is that concerning the features of the models. For example *have control*, as in (24) – which is first attested in 1888 in the *ARCHER* and in the 1830s in the *LModE-OBC* – is formed by taking *have command* as its model, as in (25). This verb is already used in EModE (Kytö 1999) and attested since 1626 in the *ARCHER*:

(24) which the defendant company **had control** (*ARCHER* 1888brew_l6a)
(25) for though 'tis granted That Lydian Omphale **had** less **command** (*ARCHER* 1626mass_d1b)

The similarity of the nominal components is in this case the driving force beyond mechanisms of direct formation promoted by analogical processes. *Control* and *command* are, indeed, very similar and belong to the same semantic field. At the same time, a partially diverse motivation worked beyond the verb *do injustice*, as in (26), which was established via analogy by taking *do justice* as its model, as in (27):

(26) "Sir, you **do** me **an injustice**, I never did you an injury." (1810s)
(27) and I should **do justice** to the publick if I did do it. (1750s)

In this case, different from the other examples discussed so far, the similarity of the nominal components is broken partially, as *justice* is the opposite of *injustice*: the fact that the nouns work as antonymous pairs is the factor determining analogy, which may also operate on forms linked by other kinds of semantic relations. The existence of analogical processes is an important factor when examining changes affecting CPs of LModE, which proves that this is a time still characterized by innovation, but it also assimilates CPs to other multi-word verbs established via analogy (Leone 2023).

64 *Processes of change*

5.4 Semantic change

CPs found in the *LModE-OBC* do not show significant changes when examined semantically, and this is due to the acquired stability of most of the combinations. However, there are a limited number of verbs that underwent lexicalization as the effect of the deletion of the articles which modifies their semantic features. This is, for example, the case of *have evidence, have information, have use, have hearing, have acquaintance, have care, take notice, take account, take place, take charge, make evidence, make haste, make resistance, make information*, and *give information*. These verbs started to be used without the article, which is a sign of increasing lexicalization, as discussed in Section 5.1, but they inevitably also increased their idiomaticity. Processes of idiomatization are often endorsed in lexicalization since combinations, whose components increase their cohesion, may tend to develop a new compositional meaning at first, which may later become more idiomatic. The close link between lexicalization and idiomatization has also inspired views that conceptualize lexicalization as including idiomatization (Bauer 1983; Wischer 2000), which is, nonetheless, not adopted in the present work. In the view taken, lexicalization may involve idiomatization or not, because new instances may also preserve their compositional status as it is the case of *have access, have effect, make agreement*, and *make proposal*, as in (28)–(29):

(28) nobody **had access** to the drawer but myself. (1770s)
(29) we **made an agreement** to meet Sunday morning (1790s)

Examination of CPs from the years 1750–1850 does not reveal significant semantic change and most of them exhibit stable use. For example, a comparison of the use of verbs like *have doubt, give notice, take notice* in the 1750s, as in (30)–(32), and 1830s, as in (33)–(35), does not suggest the existence of ongoing changes and even the lexical profile seems to be rather consolidated.

(30) I **have no doubt** about his being the man (1750s)
(31) He absconded the 7th of December, and **gave no notice** when he went away. (1750s)

(32) Did you **take notice of** the man, so as to be sure of knowing him? (1750s)
(33) they fitted him exactly, and he said he **had no doubt** they would fit (1830s)
(34) he said he would forgive me and not name it to his father if I **gave notice** to leave. (1830s)
(35) I **took no notice**; and then he said as it was a cold morning, would I object to give him some warm beer (1830s)

At the same time, there are only very rare cases of CPs characterized by semantic innovation. Specifically, the reference here is to verbs like *take place* and *have hold of*, which modify their lexical profile. *Take place* was used with nouns like *conversation, matter, robbery, illuminations*, as in (36), then in the 1830s it occurred with *accident, alternation, examination, inquest, rush, struggle, scuffle*, as in (37)–(38):

(36) I understood you to say, that this conversation **took place** in the public-house? (1790s)
(37) but I was never informed when the inquest **took place**. (1830s)
(38) about two yards from where the struggle **took place** (1830s)

There is an extension of the linguistic profile and *take place* seems to combine with an increasing number of nouns, which are in almost all cases abstract nouns in the 1830s.

Similarly, *have hold of* endorsed a path leading toward semantic renewal linked to the extension of the lexical profile. It was used with pronouns or nouns especially referring to humans first, and then it increased its uses with words denoting concrete entities like *my coat* and *the other hand*, as reported in examples (39)–(41):

(39) I **had hold of** the prisoner, and I ran the chissel at him. (1750s)
(40) but he still **had hold of** my coat (1830s)
(41) and his hand was between his thighs I **had hold of** the other hand (1830s)

Processes of change

There are no other components that can prove the existence of further semantic changes. The limited number of cases and the nature of the semantic innovation are, however, insightful because they demonstrate that the CPs of LModE are not completely conventionalized and that other processes, in addition to idiomatization, were operative at that time.

6 Conclusion

The present study has described CPs over the years 1750–1850 by querying the *LModE-OBC*, which is a corpus including transcriptions of trials giving access to spoken language predating the invention of audio-recording technology. The spoken dimension, as suggested, is an informative area of analysis when the intention is to depict the incipit of change that only after conventionalization is included in written texts.

The focus has been on the description of the linguistic behavior of CPs and the identification of processes of change affecting these verbs over the century 1750–1850. The study is, in this respect, parallel to that undertaken by Leone (2023) on multi-word verbs including phrasal verbs, prepositional verbs, and phrasal-prepositional verbs over the LModE time and further investigation of works on CPs of early periods like the studies undertaken by Kytö (1999) and Wang (2019), which focused on EModE.

The examination of the frequency of use of CPs has revealed that they are relatively frequent in the data which confirms the trend already attested in EModE creating a line of continuity between these periods. Specifically, CPs exhibit a declining trend up to the 1810s when they increase their frequency. The existence of variation in the use of the bases *do*, *give*, *have*, *make*, and *take* corroborates ongoing changes which are confirmed by the TTR expressing the degree of productivity of the bases: *have*, *do*, and *make* show the highest rates, meaning that they are prone to the formation of new CPs. Examination of the degree of productivity assimilates the results with those reported by Leone (2023) examining other multi-word verbs since the bases vary in their ability to combine with nominal parts over the decades.

68 Conclusion

Moreover, similarly to other periods, CPs exhibit phraseological variation, and often two or more CPs stand in paradigmatic competition. The declining use or obsolescence of one of the alternatives is linked to the phenomenon of layering favoring the retraction of one of the alternatives. Stability and change also feature the syntactic uses of CPs which occur in their passive form in a few cases consolidating a linguistic behavior already observed in early times. At the same time, CPs prefer the V+Ø+N pattern in LModE, which contrasts the V+D+N of PDE, granting to the LModE time the status of transition stage.

When considering the processes of change affecting CPs, the present study has provided evidence that these verbs may be seen as both lexicalized and grammaticalized as already proposed by Trousdale (2008). The increasing boundness of some nouns favored by the deletion of the determiner entails the existence of grammaticalization. In contrast, the univerbation of the components and increasing internal cohesion are signs of ongoing lexicalization. The components are involved in processes of semantic reanalysis reshaping the meaning of the combination. Signs of lexicalization also emerge from observation of CPs that exhibit variation in the use of the preposition, and gradual retraction of one of them. CPs of the years 1750–1850 are also characterized by analogical processes promoting the direct formation of new instances which were established as coinages working as members of the group of CPs.

The findings discussed in this book work as a further contribution to knowledge of CPs and their diachronical development. The results may be contextualized within research on the LModE time and give support to the current debate around the status of this period as characterized by both stability and change (Kytö et al. 2006; Culpeper 2015; Hundt 2014). The characterization of the history of CPs from the years 1750–1850 as linked to processes of grammaticalization, lexicalization, and analogy suggests the close link between these verbs and other multi-word verbs. At the same time, the common features CPs share with CPs of the early times contribute to a conceptualization of their history as based on cyclical processes. More generally, the results may inform studies on the verb system over time and be used comparatively to evaluate the extent to which verbs share common or divergent histories.

The results are, however, far from being exhaustive but open new research paths that will be the object of future investigations. The study does not touch on topics like the pragmatic uses of CPs, and

Conclusion 69

sociolinguistic aspects which may influence the history of these verbs. Moreover, the analysis revealed the existence of discrepancies in the use of CPs between EModE as examined by Claridge (2000) and LModE which have been linked to the diverse nature of the text types included in the corpora. Future research will include the evaluation of CPs in multi-genre corpora including texts from LModE to evaluate whether and the extent to which the written and spoken dimensions influence the use of CPs and their patterns over the years 1750–1850.

Appendix

List of composite predicates

DO
act
action
assignment
benefit
damage
deal
deed
endeavour
execution
favour
garden
harm
injury
injustice
job
justice
robbery
service
story
suspicion
work

GIVE
acceptance
account
affirmation
air
alarm
answer
breakfast
character
charge
countenance
credit
cut
description
difference
dinner
direction
dislike
ear
education
encouragement
endorsement
evidence
fall
friend
guarantee
hold
information
instruction
intimation
invitation
judgment
kick
liberty
lift
memorandum
motion
option
order
permission
petition
possession
price
proof
provocation
push
reason
reference
refreshment
reply
reward
rise
satisfaction
scream
security
service
stroke
suspicion
testimony
time
trouble
undertaking
verdict
voice
warning
way
word

appearance	notice	work
assault	offence	**HAVE**
assistance	opinion	access
blow		trust
account	hearing	use
acquaintance	hesitation	view
advantage	hold	warning
advice	honour	warrant
allowance	hurt	wash
answer	idea	way
appearance	impression	word
appointment	inclination	
apprehension	information	**MAKE**
assistance	intention	accusation
belief	intercourse	agreement
breakfast	interest	alarm
care	knowledge	allowance
cause	look	alternation
charge	loss	amend
command	luck	answer
communication	malice	apology
compassion	management	appearance
concern	meeting	application
confidence	mercy	appointment
confirmation	mind	arrangment
connection	misfortune	assault
consultation	mistake	attempt
control	mistrust	blow
conveniency	notice	capture
conversation	objection	cast
credit	occasion	cause
custody	opinion	charge
cut	patience	claim
deal	pleasure	communication
dealing	possession	compensation
demand	presence	complaint
description	quarrel	confession
design	question	crash
dinner	reason	declaration
discourse	recollection	defence
disorder	recourse	demand
dispute	relation	demur
dominion	satisfaction	difference
doubt	sense	discovery
effect	share	discussion
endorsement	sight	disturbance
entry	struggle	

72 Appendix

evidence	supper	doubt
fall	suspicion	effort
fire	talk	enquiry
fit	tendency	entrance
entry	practice	way
escape	promise	word
evidence	proposal	
example	proposition	**TAKE**
excuse	protestation	account
experiment	purchase	advantage
fire	remark	advice
flute	reply	aim
frame	representation	breakfast
haste	resistance	care
hit	restitution	charge
impression	robbery	compassion
information	room	deal
inquiry	run	effect
knock	rush	hold
light	satisfaction	impression
mark	scruple	liberty
memorandum	search	measure
mention	secret	notice
mistake	start	observation
motion	statement	opinion
noise	step	part
note	stop	place
objection	stroke	possession
observation	struggle	share
odds	threat	situation
offer	use	trial
omission	vow	trouble
part	water	walk
point		warning

References

Ädel, Annelie. 2021. Corpus compilation. In Magali Paquot & Stefan Th. Gries (eds.), *A Practical Handbook of Corpus Linguistics*, 3–24. Cham: Springer.
Akimoto, Minoji. 1989. *A Study of Verbo-Nominal Structures in English*. Tokyo: Shinozaki Shorin.
Akimoto, Minoji. 1999. Collocations and idioms in Late Modern English. In Laurel J. Brinton & Minoji Akimoto (eds.), *Collocational and Idiomatic Aspects of Composite Predicates in the History of English*, 207–238. Amsterdam & Philadelphia: John Benjamins Publishing Company.
Akimoto, Minoji & Laurel J. Brinton. 1999. The origin of the composite predicates in Old English. In Laurel J. Brinton & Minoji Akimoto (eds.), *Collocational and Idiomatic Aspects of Composite Predicates in the History of English*, 21–58. Amsterdam & Philadelphia: John Benjamins Publishing Company.
Algeo, John. 1995. Have a look at the expanded predicate. In Bas Aarts & Charles F. Meyer (eds.), *The Verb in Contemporary English: Theory and Description*, 203–217. Cambridge: Cambridge University Press.
Alonso, Roberto Torre, & Gema Maiz Villalta. 2014. Hapax legomena and the productivity of the Old English weak verb suffixes. *Nordic Journal of English Studies* 13.3, 188–211.
Anttila, Raimo. 1989. *Historical and Comparative Linguistics*. Amsterdam & Philadelphia: John Benjamins Publishing Company.
Baker, James. 2016. The Covent Garden Old price riots: Protest and justice in Late-Georgian London. *Open Library of Humanities* 2.1, e4.
Baker, James. 2017. *The Business of Satirical Prints in Late-Georgian England*. Cham: Palgrave Macmillan.
Bauer, Laurie. 1983. *English Word-Formation*. Cambridge: Cambridge University Press.
Beattie, John M. 2012. *The First English Detectives: The Bow Street Runners and the Policing of London, 1750-1840*. Oxford: Oxford University Press.

References

Biber, Douglas & Edward Finegan. 1992. The linguistic evolution of five written and speech-based English genres from the 17th to the 20th centuries. In Matti Rissanen, Ossi Ihalainen, Terttu Nevalainen & Irma Taavitsainen (eds.), *History of Englishes. New Methods and Interpretations in Historical Linguistics*, 688–704. Berlin & New York: Mouton de Gruyter.

Biber, Douglas. 1993. Representativeness in corpus design. *Literary and Linguistic Computing* 8.4, 243–258.

Biber, Douglas, Susan Conrad & Randi Reppen. 1998. *Corpus Linguistics. Investigating Language Structure and Use*. Cambridge: Cambridge University Press.

Biber, Douglas, Stig Johansson, Geoffrey Leech, Susan Conrad & Edward Finegan. 1999. *Longman Grammar of Spoken and Written English*. Harlow: Pearson Education.

Biber, Douglas, Stig Johansson, Geoffrey Leech, Susan Conrad & Edward Finegan. 2021. *Grammar of Spoken and Written English*. Amsterdam & Philadelphia: John Benjamins Publishing Company.

Bolinger, Dwight. 1971. *The Phrasal Verb in English*. Cambridge, MA: Harvard University Press.

Boulton, Jeremy. 2007. Welfare Systems and the Parish Nurse in Early Modern London, 1650-1725. *Family & Community History* 10.2, 127–151.

Brezina, Vaclav. 2018. *Statistics in Corpus Linguistics*. Cambridge: Cambridge University Press.

Brinton, Laurel J. 1988. *The Development of English Aspectual System. Aspectualizers and Post-verbal Particles*. Cambridge: Cambridge University Press.

Brinton, Laurel J. 1996. Attitudes toward increasing segmentalization: Complex and phrasal verbs in English. *Journal of English Linguistics* 24.3, 186–205.

Brinton, Laurel. 2008. 'Where Lexis and Grammar Meet': Composite predicates in English. In Elena Seoane & Mariá José López-Couso (eds.), *Theoretical and Empirical Issues in Grammaticalization*, 33–53. Amsterdam & Philadelphia: John Benjamins Publishing Company.

Brinton, Laurel J. 2011. The grammaticalization of complex predicates. In Heiko Narrog & Bernd Heine (eds.), *The Oxford Handbook of Grammaticalization*, 559–569. Oxford: Oxford University Press.

Brinton, Laurel J. & Minoji Akimoto (eds.). 1999. *Collocational and Idiomatic Aspects of Composite Predicates in the History of English*. Amsterdam & Philadelphia: John Benjamins Publishing Company.

Brinton, Laurel J. & Elizabeth Closs Traugott. 2005. *Lexicalization and Language Change*. Cambridge: Cambridge University Press.

Cattell, Ray. 1984. *Composite Predicates in English*. Sydney: Academic Press.

Claridge, Claudia. 2000. *Multi-word Verbs in Early Modern English: A Corpus-based Study*. Amsterdam & Atlanta, GA: Rodopi.

References 75

Claridge, Claudia & Merja Kytö. 2014. I had lost sight of them then for a bit, but I went on pretty fast. In Irma Taavitsainen, Andreas H. Jucker & Jukka Touminen (eds.), *Diachronic Corpus Pragmatics*, 29–52. Amsterdam & Philadelphia: John Benjamins Publishing Company.

Cowie, Anthony Paul. 1998. Introduction. In Anthony Paul Cowie (ed.), *Phraseology: Theory, Analysis and Applications*, 1–20. Oxford: Oxford University Press.

Culpeper, Jonathan. 2005. *History of English*. London & New York: Routledge.

Culpeper, Jonathan & Merja Kytö. 2010. *Early Modern English Dialogues: Spoken Interaction as Writing*. Cambridge: Cambridge University Press.

Curme, George O. 1931. *A Grammar of the English Language in Three Volumes. Vol. III. Syntax*. Boston: D. C. Heath and Company.

Danchev, Andrei. 1992. The evidence for analytic and synthetic developments in English. In Matti Rissanen, Ossi Ihalainen, Terttu Nevalainen & Irma Taavitsainen (eds.), *History of Englishes: New Methods and Interpretations in Historical Linguistics*, 25–41. Berlin & New York: De Gruyter Mouton.

Denison, David. 1981. *Aspects of the History of English Group-verbs, with particular attention to the Syntax of the ORMULUM*. Oxford: University of Oxford PhD Dissertation. www.escholar.manchester.ac.uk/uk-ac-manscw:74782 (accessed 8 January 2016)

Elenbaas, Marion. 2007. *The Synchronic and Diachronic Syntax of the English Verb-Particle Combination*. Utrecht: LOT. www.lotpublications.nl/Documents/149_fulltext.pdf (accessed 20 March 2016)

Fischer, Olga. 2007. *Morphosyntactic Change. Functional and Formal Perspectives*. Oxford & New York: Oxford University Press.

Fraser, Bruce. 1974. *The Verb-particle Combination in English*. Tokyo: Taishukan Publishing Company.

Fitzmaurice, Susan M. & Taavitsainen, Irma. 2007 (eds.). *Methods in Historical Pragmatics*. Berlin & New York: De Gruyter Mouton.

Görlach, Manfred. 1991 [1978]. *Introduction to Early Modern English*. Cambridge: Cambridge University Press.

Granger, Sylviane & Magali Paquot. 2008. Disentangling the phraseological web. In Sylviane Granger & Fanny Meunier (eds.), *Phraseology. An Interdisciplinary Perspective*, 27–49. Amsterdam & Philadelphia: John Benjamins Publishing Company.

Gries, Stefan Th. 2008. Phraseology and linguistic theory: A brief survey. In Sylviane Granger & Fanny Meunier (eds.), *Phraseology: An Interdisciplinary Perspective*, 3–25. Amsterdam & Philadelphia: John Benjamins Publishing Company.

Hardie, Andrew. 2012. CQPweb – combining power, flexibility and usability in a corpus analysis tool. *International Journal of Corpus Linguistics* 17.3, 380–409.

References

Haspelmath, Martin. 2004. On directionality in language change with particular reference to grammaticalization. In Olga Fischer (ed.), *Up and Down the Cline. The Nature of Grammaticalization,* 17–44. Amsterdam & Philadelphia: John Benjamins Publishing Company.

Hickey, Raymond. 2010. Preface. In Raymond Hickey (ed.), *Eighteenth-century English. Ideology and Change.* Cambridge: Cambridge University Press.

Hiltunen, Risto. 1983. *The Decline of the Prefixes and the Beginnings of the English Phrasal Verb: The Evidence from some Old and Early Middle English Texts.* Turku: Turun Yliopisto.

Hiltunen, Risto. 1999. Verbal phrases and phrasal verbs in Early Modern English. In Laurel J. Brinton & Minoji Akimoto (eds.), *Collocational and Idiomatic Aspects of Composite Predicates in the History of English,* 133–166. Amsterdam & Philadelphia: John Benjamins Publishing Company.

Hopper, Paul J. & Elizabeth Closs Traugott. 2003 [1993]. *Grammaticalization,* 2nd edn. Cambridge: Cambridge University Press.

Huber, Magnus. 2007. The Old Bailey Proceedings, 1674–1834: Evaluating and annotating a corpus of 18th- and 19th-century spoken English. In Anneli Meurman-Solin & Arja Nurmi (eds.), *Annotating Variation and Change* (Studies in Variation, Contacts and Change in English 1). www.helsinki.fi/ varieng/journal/volumes/01/huber/ (accessed 16 January 2012)

Huber, Magnus. 2017. Structural and sociolinguistic factors conditioning the choice of relativizers in Late Modern English: A diachronic study based on the Old Bailey Corpus. *Nordic Journal of English Studies* 16.1, 74–119.

Huber, Magnus, Magnus Nissel & Karin Puga. 2016. *Old Bailey Corpus 2.0.* hdl:11858/00-246C-0000-0023-8CFB-2

Huddleston, Rodney & Geoffrey K. Pullum. 2002. *The Cambridge Grammar of the English Language.* Cambridge: Cambridge University Press.

Hundt, Marianne. 2014. Introduction: Late Modern English syntax in its linguistic and socio-historical context. In Marianne Hundt (ed.), *Late Modern English Syntax,* 1–10. Cambridge: Cambridge University Press.

Iglesias-Rábade, Luis. 2001. Composite predicates in Middle English with the verbs *nimen* and *taken. Studia Neophilologica* 72.2, 143–163.

Jespersen, Otto. 1942. *A Modern English Grammar on Historical Principles. Part VI: Morphology.* With the assistance of P. Christophersen, N. Haislund & K. Schibsbye. London: George Allen & Unwin. Copenhagen: Ejnar Munksgaard.

Jucker, Andreas. 1995 (eds.). *Historical Pragmatics. Pragmatic Developments in the History of English.* Amsterdam & Philadephia: John Benjamins Publishing Company.

Klaeber, Friedrich. 1943. Zum germanischen Sprachstil: Das Nomen. *Archiv für das Studium der neueren und Literaturen* 183, 73–94.

Koskenniemi, Inna. 1977. On the use of verbal phrases of the type 'to take revenge' in English Renaissance Drama. *Poetica* 7, 80–90.

Kruisinga, Etsko. 1931 [1911]. *A Handbook of Present-Day English. Part II: English Accidence and Syntax*. Groningen: P. Noordhoff.

Kytö, Merja. 1999. Collocational and idiomatic aspects of verbs in Early Modern English. In Laurel J. Brinton & Minoji Akimoto (eds.), *Collocational and Idiomatic Aspects of Composite Predicates in the History of English*, 167–206. Amsterdam & Philadelphia: John Benjamins Publishing Company.

Kytö, Merja, Mats Rydén & Erik Smitterberg. 2006. Introduction: Exploring nineteenth-century English-past and present perspectives. In Merja Kytö, Mats Rydén & Erik Smitterberg (eds.), *Nineteenth-century English. Stability and Change*, 1–16. Cambridge: Cambridge University Press.

Kytö, Merja & Terry Walker. 2006. *Guide to A Corpus of English Dialogues 1560–1760* (Studia Anglistica Upsaliensia 130). Uppsala: Acta Universitatis Upsaliensis.

Kytö, Merja, Terry Walker & Peter Grund. 2007. English witness depositions 1560-1760: An electronic text edition. *ICAME Journal* 31, 65–85.

Lavidas, Nikolaos & Alexander Bergs. 2020. On historical language contact in English and its types: State of art and new directions. *Linguistic Vanguard* 6.2, 20200010.

Leone, Ljubica. 2016a. Phrasal verbs and analogical generalization in Late Modern Spoken English. *ICAME Journal* 40.1, 39–62.

Leone, Ljubica. 2016b. Aspectual and idiomatic properties of the particle *on* in Late Modern Spoken English. *Topics in Linguistics* 17.1, 64–80.

Leone, Ljubica. 2019. Context-induced reinterpretation of phraseological verbs. Phrasal verbs in Late Modern English. In Gloria C. Pastor & Ruslan Mitkov (eds.), *Computational and Corpus-Based Phraseology, Third International Conference, Europhras 2019, Malaga, Spain, September 25-27. 2019, Conference Proceedings*, 253–267. Cham, Switzerland: Springer Nature.

Leone, Ljubica. 2022. The particle *forth* during the Early Modern English period: linguistic interferences with the particles *on* and *out*. Studia Neophilologica.

Leone, Ljubica. 2023. *Multi-word Verbs in the Late Modern English Period (1750-1850): A Corpus-Based Study*. Munich: Lincom.

Live, Anna H. 1973. The take-have phrasal verb in English. *Linguistics* 95, 31–50.

Lyons, John. 1968. *Introduction to Theoretical Linguistics*. Cambridge: Cambridge University Press.

Matsumoto, Meiko. 1999. Composite predicates in Middle English. In Laurel J. Brinton & Minoji Akimoto (eds.), *Collocational and Idiomatic Aspects of Composite Predicates in the History of English*, 59–95. Amsterdam & Philadelphia: John Benjamins Publishing Company.

Matsumoto, Meiko. 2005. The historical development and functional characteristics of composite predicates with *have* and *take* in English. *English Studies* 86.5, 439–456.

Matsumoto, Meiko. 2007. The verb *have* and *take* in composite predicates and phrasal verbs. *Studia Neophilologica* 79.2, 159–170.

Matsumoto, Meiko. 2008. *From Simple Verbs to Periphrastic Expressions. The Historical Development of Composite Predicates, Phrasal Verbs, and Related Constructions in English.* Bern: Peter Lang.

McEnery, Tony & Andrew Hardie. 2012. *Corpus Linguistics*. Cambridge: Cambridge University Press.

Mitchell, Bruce. 1985. *Old English Syntax*. Oxford: Clarendon.

Mitchell, Bruce & Fred C. Robinson. 1992. *A Guide to Old English*. 5th edn. Oxford & Cambridge, MA: Basil Blackwell.

Moralejo Gárate, Teresa. 2002. Composite predicates and modification flexibility in Middle English. *Atlantis* 24.1, 173–187.

Mugglestone, Lynda. 2006. *The Oxford History of English*. Oxford: Oxford University Press.

Murphy, Lynne M. 2003. *Semantic Relations and the Lexicon. Antonymy, Synonymy, and Other Paradigms*. Cambridge: Cambridge University Press.

Nevalainen, Terttu. 2006. *An Introduction to Early Modern English*. Oxford: Oxford University Press.

Nickel, Gerhard. 1968. Complex verbal structures in English. *International Review of Applied Linguistics* 6.1, 1–21.

OED = *Oxford English Dictionary*. Online: www.oed.com/

Olsson, Yngve. 1961. *On the Syntax of the English Verb, with Specific Reference to* Have a Look *and Similar Complex Structures*. Göteborg: Elanders Boktryckeri Aktiebolag.

Poutsma, Hendrik. 1926. *A Grammar of Late Modern English for the Use of Continental, especially Dutch, students. Part II: The Parts of Speech. Section II: The Verb and the Particles.* Groningen: P. Noordhoff.

Quirk, Randolph, Sidney Greenbaum, Geoffrey Leech & Jan Svartvik. 1985. *A Comprehensive Grammar of the English Language*. London: Longman.

Rayson, Paul & Roger, Garside. 2000. Comparing Corpora using Frequency Profiling. In Adam Kilgarrif & Tony Berber Sardinha (eds.), *The Workshop on Comparing Corpora*, 1–6, Hong Kong, China. Association for Computational Linguistics.

Rayson, Paul, Damon Berridge & Brian Francis. 2004. Extending the Conchran rule for the comparison of word frequencies between corpora. In Gérald Purnelle, Cédrick Fairon & Anne Dister (eds.), *Le poids des mots: Proceedings of the 7th International Conference on Statistical*

References

Analysis of Textual Data (JADT 2004), Louvain-la-Neuve, Belgium, March 10-12, 2004, 926–936. Louvain: Presses Universitaires de Louvain.

Rayson, Paul. 2008. Log-likelihood calculator. UCREL web server. https://ucrel.lancs.ac.uk/llwizard.html

Rodríguez-Puente, Paula. 2016.Tracking down phrasal verbs in the spoken language of the past: Late Modern English in focus. *English Language and Linguistics* 21.1, 69–97.

Rodríguez-Puente, Paula. 2019. *The English Phrasal Verb, 1650-present. History, Stylistic Drifts, and Lexicalization*. Cambridge: Cambridge University Press.

Rodríguez-Puente, Paula & María Obaya-Cueli. 2022. Phrasal verbs in Early Modern English spoken language: A colloquialization conspiracy? *English Language & Linguistics* 26.4, 807–831.

Sánchez Rousa, María Teresa. 2003. Colloquial language in the *Wakefield plays*: composite predicates. *Revista Canaria De Estudios Ingleses* 46, 183–198.

Scott, Mike. 2013. WordSmith Tools. Version 6.0. Oxford: Oxford University Press.

Siemund, Rainer & Claudia Claridge. 1997. The Lampeter Corpus of Early Modern English Tracts. *ICAME Journal* 21, 61–70.

Sinclair, John. 1991. *Corpus, Concordance, Collocation*. Oxford: Oxford University Press.

Stein, Gabriele & Randolph Quirk. 1991. On having a look in a corpus. In Karin Aijmer & Bengt Altenberg (eds.), *English Corpus Linguistics: Studies in Honour of Jan Svartvik*, 197–203. London: Longman.

Svensson, Maria Helena. 2008. A very complex criterion of fixedness: Non-compositionality. In Sylviane Granger & Fanny Meunier (eds.), *Phraseology. An Interdisciplinary Perspective*, 81–93. Amsterdam & Philadelphia: John Benjamins Publishing Company.

Tanabe, Harumi. 1999. Composite predicates and phrasal verbs in *The Paston Letters*. In Laurel J. Brinton & Minoji Akimoto (eds.), *Collocational and Idiomatic Aspects of Composite Predicates in the History of English*, 97–132. Amsterdam & Philadelphia: John Benjamins Publishing Company.

The Proceedings of the Old Bailey Online, 1674–1913. www.oldbaileyonline.org/

Thim, Stefan. 2012. *Phrasal verbs. The English Verb-particle Construction and its History*. Berlin & Boston: De Gruyter Mouton.

Tieken-Boon van Ostade, Ingrid. 2009. *An Introduction to Late Modern English*. Edinburgh: Edinburgh University Press.

Traugott, Elizabeth Closs. 1999. A historical overview of complex predicate types. In Brinton, Laurel J. & Minoji Akimoto (eds.), *Collocational and Idiomatic Aspects of Composite Predicates in the History of English*, 239–260. Amsterdam & Philadelphia: John Benjamins Publishing Company.

Trousdale, Graeme. 2008. Constructions in grammaticalization and lexicalization: Evidence from the history of a composite predicate construction in English. In Graeme Trousdale & Nikolas Gisborne (eds.), *Constructional Approaches to English Grammar*, 33–70. Berlin & New York: De Gruyter Mouton.

Trudgill, Peter. 2016. Contact-related processes of change in the early history of English. In Merja Kytö & Päivi Pahta (eds.), *The Cambridge Handbook of Historical Linguistics*, 318–334. Cambridge: Cambridge University Press.

van Gelderen, Elly. 2006. *A History of English Language*. Amsterdam & Philadelphia: John Benjamins Publishing Company.

van Gelderen, Elly. 2013. The linguistic cycle and the language faculty. *Language and Linguistics Compass* 7.4, 233–250.

van Gelderen, Elly. 2018. *The Diachrony of Verb Meaning. Aspect and Argument Structure*. New York & London: Routledge.

Visser, Federik Th. 1963–1973. *An Historical Syntax of the English Language*. Leiden: E.J. Brill.

Wang, Ying. 2019. A corpus-based study of composite predicates in Early Modern English dialogues. *Journal of Historical Pragmatics* 20.1, 20–50.

Wierzbicka, Anna. 1982. Why Can You *have a drink* When You Can't *have an eat*? *Language* 58.4, 753–799.

Wischer, Ilse. 2000. Grammaticalization versus lexicalization: 'Methinks' there is some confusion. In Olga Fischer, Anette Rosenbach & Dieter Stein (eds.), *Pathways of Change. Grammaticalization in English*, 355–370. Amsterdam & Philadelphia: John Benjamins Publishing Company.

Yáñez-Bouza, Nuria. 2011a. ARCHER past and present (1990–2010). *ICAME Journal* 35, 205–236.

Yáñez-Bouza, Nuria. 2011b. *ARCHER past and present (1990–2011)*. Poster presented at the 32nd Conference of the International Computer Archive of Modern and Medieval English (ICAME 32), Oslo, 1–5 June 2011.

Index

Note: Page numbers in *italics* indicate figures and in **bold** indicate tables on the corresponding pages.

Akimoto, Minoji 14, 15–16, 21–22, 35, 55, 58
analytic language, English as 21
ARCHER corpus *see Representative Corpus of Historical English Registers, A (ARCHER)*
articles and determiners 44–46, **45**

base verbs in composite predicates *30*, 30–31
Biber, Douglas 10
body nouns in composite predicates 22–23
Bolinger, Dwight 23
Brinton, Laurel J. 4, 10, 14, 15–16, 20–22, 31, 35, 56, 59

Cattell, Ray 23
Claridge, Claudia 10, 15, 22, 69; on degree of formality 25–26; on semantic features of composite predicates 54; on spread of composite predicates in Early Modern English 18–20
colloquiality 19, 26
complex verbs 2–3
composite predicates: articles and determiners in 44–46, **45**; base verbs in *30*, 30–31; body nouns in 22–23; coinage of new 61–63; concordance-based analysis of selected 11; definition of 1; distribution of 25–30, *27*, *29*; in Early Modern English 18–21; grammaticality of 3–4, *4*, 23, 55–59; idiomatic meaning in 17–18, 22; internal modification of **47**, 47–50; lexicalization and 3–4, *4*, 20–21, 55–59; linguistic overview of 4–6; list of 70–72; literature on 6–7; origins in Old English and Middle English 6–7, 14–18; passivization and 51–53, **52**; phraseological constituency of 2–3; phraseological variation across the years 1750-1850 31–34, **33**; phraseological variation and layering between alternative prepositions 59–61; in Present Day English 23–24; processes of change of (*see* processes of change of composite predicates); productivity of 37–40, **38**, **39**; quantitative analysis of 11–12; selection of 10–11; semantic features of 53–54; stability and change of (*see* stability and change of composite predicates); stable 41–42; syntactic patterns of

42–44; use of deverbal nouns with more than one verb in 34–37, **36**; use of plural forms of 50–51
Construction Grammar framework 23–24
Corpus of English Dialogues (CED) 10, 20–21, 30
CPs *see* composite predicates
crime and criminal justice descriptions 8
Curme, George O. 23

Denison, David 6
deverbal nouns 1, 34–37, **36**
Dictionary of Old English 15

Early Modern English (EModE) 67; base verbs in 30–31; colloquiality in 26; distributional properties in 26–30, *27*, *29*; semantic features of composite predicates in 54; spread of composite predicates in 18–21; use of plural forms in 50–51
establishment of composite predicates 14–18

Finegan, Edward 10
Fraser, Bruce 23

grammaticalization 3–4, *4*, 20–21, 55–59
Gries, Stefan Th. 2

Helsinki Corpus of English Texts 10, 39, 46
Hiltunen, Risto 6, 18–19, 47

idiomatic meaning in composite predicates 17–18, 22
internal modification of composite predicates **47**, 47–50

Koskenniemi, Inna 18
Kruisinga, Etsko 23
Kytö, Merja 37, 39, 67; on coinage of new composite predicates 61; on colloquiality 19; on composite predicates of the Early Modern English time 18; on internal modification 47; on multiple use of nouns 36; on plural forms 50, 51; on selections of composite predicates for analysis 10; on semantic features of composite predicates 54

Lampeter Corpus 19–20, 26
Late Modern English (LModE): base verbs in 30–31; colloquiality in 26; distributional properties in 26–30, *27*, *29*; passivization in 52–53; stability and change in 21–23; syntactic patterns in 43–44; use of deverbal nouns in 35–36
Late Modern English-Old Bailey Corpus (LModE-OBC) 67; articles and determiners in 45–46; on coinage of new composite predicates 61; compilation of 7–9; corpus architecture and size **9**, 9–10; distribution of composite predicates in 25; on grammaticalization and lexicalization 56–57, 58; internal modification in 48; phrasal verbs in 36; phraseological variation and layering between alternative prepositions 60; semantic features of composite predicates in 53–54; stable composite predicates in 41–42
Leone, Ljubica 26, 37, 67
lexicalization 3–4, *4*, 20–21, 55–59
linguistic features of composite predicates: base verbs *30*, 30–31; distribution 25–30, *27*, *29*; phraseological variation across the years 1750-1850 31–34, **33**; productivity 37–40, **38**, **39**; use of deverbal nouns with more than one verb 34–37, **36**
Live, Anna H. 23
log-likelihood (LL) score 11–12
Lyons, John 56

Matsumoto, Meiko 16, 17–18, 22–23; on modifiers 47, 48–49
Middle English (ME) 7; establishment of composite predicates in 14–18; passivization in 53; syntactic patterns in 42–44
Middle English Dictionary (MED) 15
Mitchell, Bruce 14
modifiers, internal **47**, 47–50
Moralejo Gárate, Teresa 17, 33, 46
multi-word verbs 6, 63, 67–68; defined 1–3; development of 7, 12; internal modification of 47; in the Late Modern English period 26, 36; in the early Modern English period 22; in the Middle English period 18; in present day English 23; semantic features of 53

Nickel, Gerhard 6

Obaya-Cueli, Maria 26
Old English (OE) 6–7; establishment of composite predicates in 14–18
Oxford English Dictionary (OED) 21, 57; semantic features of composite predicates and 55
Oxford Text Archive (OTA) 18–19

passivization 51–53, **52**
Paston Letters, The 16–17, 53
phrasal-prepositional verbs 1
phrasal verbs 1
phraseological variation and layering between alternative prepositions 59–61
phraseology 3
plural forms of composite predicates 50–51
Poutsma, Hendrik 23
prepositional verbs 1
Present day English (PDE) 12; current forms and usages of composite predicates in 23–24; deverbal nouns in 16;

idiomatization in 17–18; syntactic patterns of composite predicates in 42–44
processes of change of composite predicates: coinage of new composite predicates and 61–63; grammaticalization and lexicalization 55–59; phraseological variation and layering between alternative prepositions 59–61; semantic change 64
productivity 37–40, **38**, **39**

Representative Corpus of Historical English Registers, A (ARCHER) 10, 41, 57–58; coinage of new composite predicates 62, 63
Robinson, Fred C. 14
Rodríguez-Puente, Paula 26

Sánchez Roura, Maria Teresa 17, 26, 35
semantic features 53–54
Shakespeare, William 18
Sinclair, John 3
speech-based genres 8–9
stability and change of composite predicates 41–42; articles and determiners and 44–46, **45**; internal modification and **47**, 47–50; in Late Modern English 21–23; morpho-syntactic features and 42–53; passivization and 51–53, **52**; plural forms and 50–51; semantic features and 53–54; syntactic patterns and 42–44
syntactic patterns of composite predicates 42–44
synthetic language, English as 21

Tanabe, Harumi 10, 16–17, 30, 49, 53
Traugott, Elizabeth Closs 4, 55, 56, 59
Trousdale, Graeme 59, 68
type/token ratio (TTR) 11–12, 19, 37, **38–39**, 38–40, 67

verb-adjective combinations 2
verbal phrases 2–3
verbo-nominal combinations 3
verb-prepositional phrase
 combinations 1–2
verbs: complex 2–3; multi-word
 1–2, 3, 34–37, **36**

verb-verb combinations 1
Visser, Federik Theodor 15,
 18

Wakefield Plays 26
Wang, Ying 10, 20–21, 37, 44, 45,
 55, 67

For Product Safety Concerns and Information please contact our EU
representative GPSR@taylorandfrancis.com
Taylor & Francis Verlag GmbH, Kaufingerstraße 24, 80331 München, Germany

www.ingramcontent.com/pod-product-compliance
Lightning Source LLC
Chambersburg PA
CBHW051759230426
43670CB00012B/2356